Granny's Legacy

Granny's Legacy

Recipes from the Collection of
Dorothy Helen (Hall) Stauffacher
Feb 3, 1906 – Oct 10, 1995

Enjoy & make your family legacy!
Linda Flynn

At her home
In her kitchen
Around her table......

......we learned to appreciate good food
and the value of family and friends!

Compiled and Edited by Linda L. Flynn
(Dorothy's oldest grand-daughter)
3rd edition

This book is dedicated to
my grandmother's memory
and
to my daughters.

May we pass this legacy down
through our children to future generations.

INTRODUCTION

This collection of recipes is a compilation of the three recipe boxes from Granny's house. I took the liberty of adding some personal recipes Granny had given me, which were not in her boxes.

Every effort was made to include personal notes and annotations found on the recipes. A number of recipes had red stars on them, so you will find those recipes in this book – with stars. Any notes added to the recipes have been included in italic text.

Some of the older recipes were nothing more than a listing of ingredients. So please do not be surprised, or think I omitted something when you come across these.

This third edition has some formatting changes. It is a reprint of the first two editions to accommodate requests for a copy of the book and facilitate easier printing.

For those of you who knew Granny, you already know she loved God, loved her family and loved to cook. Her faith was lived out in her daily life; she was an inspiration to far more people than I think most of us will ever imagine.

She was also a woman who was way ahead of her time. As I've gotten older, I think back upon much of the advice she gave me and realize her advice played a large role in shaping my belief system. I probably never felt the need to be involved in feminist issues because so many things those women of the '70's were fighting for – were things I took for granted given the environment I grew up in. Dorothy Stauffacher played a big part in who I am, and how I approach life.

I started this project because I wanted to ensure my children and grandchildren would have access to these recipes. I failed to realize how long it would take – or to acknowledge the journey I would take during this project. Seeing Granny's handwriting, or some of the recipes that were favorites has been quite overpowering. Many times my day's work ended on a long journey down memory lane.

For those of you who did get to personally know her, I hope you will find some favorites in this book – and that you will share them with family and friends; thus starting your own traditions of valuing good food and time spent with others.

Granny, thank you!

With love,

Linda

BREAD

★ APPLESAUCE FIG LOAF

2 cups flour
1 teaspoon baking powder
1 teaspoon baking soda
½ teaspoon cinnamon
¼ teaspoon cloves
¼ teaspoon nutmeg
1/3 cup soft butter or margarine

2/3 cup sugar
1 egg
1 teaspoon vanilla
1½ cups canned applesauce
½ cup chopped nuts
1 cup chopped dried figs

Sift flour, baking powder, soda, cinnamon, cloves and nutmeg; set aside. In large bowl, cream butter with sugar until light and fluffy. Add egg and vanilla, beating well. Gradually beat in flour mixture, just until combined. Add applesauce, nuts and dried figs. Spoon into greased loaf pan. Bake at 350 degrees about 1 hour or until done. Let stand in pan 10 minutes; cool on rack. Serve plain or with a glaze over top. Cut into thin slices.

* * * * *

BANANA BREAD

1¾ cup sifted flour
2¾ teaspoons baking powder
½ teaspoon cinnamon
1/8 teaspoon nutmeg
½ teaspoon salt
½ cup chopped nuts

1/3 cup shortening
2/3 cup sugar
2 eggs slightly beaten
1 cup mashed bananas (3 – 4)
1 cup candied fruit
¼ cup raisins

Sift dry ingredients together, add nuts and set aside. Cream shortening, add sugar and eggs and cream well. Add dry ingredients alternating with mashed bananas, stirring only enough to blend. Stir in fruit and raisins.
Pour into a greased 4 ½ x 8 ½ x 3 loaf pan. Bake at 350 degrees for 60 – 70 minutes.

* * * * *

BANANNA BREAD

2 cups flour
1 teaspoon soda
1 teaspoon baking powder
½ teaspoon salt
½ cup shortening

1 cup sugar
2 eggs
2 cups mashed ripe bananas (4 large
    bananas)

Sift flour, measure, and sift 3 times with dry ingredients. Cream shortening and sugar thoroughly. Add eggs one at a time. Beat well after each addition. Mix in dry ingredients and bananas alternately.

Bake at 350 degrees in a greased 2 lb. Bread pan, about 1¼ hour or until firm.

If desired you can add:
1 cup candied fruit
1 cup raisins

* * * * *

BANANNA BREAD

2 cups all purpose flour
1 teaspoon baking powder
½ teaspoon baking soda
½ teaspoon salt
1½ cup mashed fully ripe bananas

2½ cups Kellogg's 40% Bran flakes cereal
½ cup margarine or butter, softened
¾ cup sugar
2 eggs
½ cup coarsely chopped nuts

Stir together flour, baking powder, soda and salt. Combine mashed bananas and cereal; let stand 2 minutes. In large mixing bowl, beat margarine and sugar. Beat in eggs and cereal mixture. Stir in flour mixture and nuts. Spread in greased 9 x 5 x 3 inch loaf pan. Bake at 350 degrees about 1 hour or until tests done. Let cool 10 minutes before removing from pan. Cool completely.

* * * * *

★ CARROT BREAD

From Pearl Stauffacher

Sift together:
1½ cup sifted flour
1 teaspoon baking powder
1 teaspoon soda

¼ teaspoon salt
1 teaspoon cinnamon

Combine in a mixing bowl:
¾ cup oil
1 cup sugar

Mix well. Add one at a time – 2 eggs. Beat well after each addition. Add dry ingredients, beating until smooth after each addition.

Add:
1 cup finely grated carrots
¼ cup finely chopped walnuts

Blend well. Turn into a well-greased loaf pan (9 x 5 x 3). Bake in a moderate oven (350 degrees) for 55 – 60 minutes.

Remove from pan and cool on rack.

* * * * *

CRANBERRY WHEAT GERM BREAD

2 cups sifted enriched flour
1 cup sugar
2 teaspoons baking powder
½ teaspoon baking soda
1½ teaspoons salt
1 cup halved raw cranberries
2 tablespoons salad oil

½ cup chopped pecans
½ cup wheat germ
3 tablespoons grated orange peel
1 egg slightly beaten
½ cup orange juice
¼ cup warm water

Mix and sift flour, sugar, baking powder, soda and salt. Stir in cranberry halves, pecans, wheat germ and orange peel. Combine egg, orange juice, water and oil. Add to flour mixture. Stir just enough to moisten ingredients. Spoon into greased loaf pan (9 x 5 x 3 inches). Bake at 350 degrees for 50 – 60 minutes or until done. Cool in pan 5 minutes; remove from pan. Finish cooling on rack.

* * * * *

4

★ FABULOUS APPLE-RAISIN LOAF

From WI State Journal – Sept 24, 1967

½ cup apple juice
1 cup canned applesauce
2/3 cup seedless raisins
2/3 cup chopped walnuts
1 cup brown sugar
2¾ cups all purpose flour
1 tablespoon baking powder

1 teaspoon baking soda
1 teaspoon salt
¾ teaspoon mace
¾ teaspoon nutmeg
1 egg, beaten
2 tablespoons melted butter

Combine apple juice, applesauce, raisins, walnuts and brown sugar. Sift together flour, baking powder, baking soda, salt, mace and nutmeg. Add dry ingredients to fruit mixture. Stir in beaten egg and melted butter. Pour into a 9 x 5 x 3 inch greased loaf pan. Bake in a moderate oven (350 degrees) for 1 hour and 15 minutes. Cool 10 minutes. Remove from pan. Cool on wire rack.

＊ ＊ ＊ ＊ ＊

★ GUMDROP BREAD

Big gumdrops

Cream:
1 cup butter

Add:
2 cups sugar
4 eggs – beat slightly

Mix:
4 cups sifted flour
1 teaspoon salt
2 teaspoon baking powder

2 teaspoon cinnamon
1 teaspoon nutmeg

Add dry ingredients alternately with 1 cup milk. Fold in 1 pound cut colored gum drops, ¾ cup nutmeats. Bake 50 – 60 minutes at 325 degrees.

＊ ＊ ＊ ＊ ＊

NUT LOAF

Easy to prepare and wonderful eating. Make enough for leftovers. It makes a great after school snack.

Cover 1½ cups of wheat germ with nut milk and let the wheat germ absorb all the milk it will take up.

Drain slightly. Place in mixing bowl and mix with 1 cup chopped walnuts, one chopped onion, one chopped green pepper, the juice of one lemon, 1 tablespoon cold-pressed corn oil and one egg, well beaten. Form into loaf. Place in pan and bake at 325 degrees, about 30 minutes. Serve with tomato sauce.

＊ ＊ ＊ ＊ ＊

★ PEAR BREAD

Each stewed:
1 cup prunes
1 cup apricots
1 cup dried apples
1 cup dried pears

1½ cup sugar
1 heaping tablespoon lard
1 egg
½ cup cold water or red grape wine
½ teaspoon salt
1 teaspoon soda
1 teaspoon baking powder

1 cup raisins
1 cup nutmeats
1 teaspoon cinnamon
½ teaspoon allspice
1 teaspoon anise seed or flavoring
About 4 cups flour

Bake in slow oven (325 degrees) for about 1 hour.

★ ★ ★ ★ ★

★ PEAR BREAD

From Mother (Victor Stauffacher's mother)

2½ pounds pears (prunes)
1 pound apricots
1 pound peaches
1 pound dried apples
3 lemons (juice)
½ quart walnut meats
½ quart citron
1½ tablespoons cinnamon

½ tablespoon cloves
½ tablespoon allspice
½ tablespoon nutmeg
5 Cents powdered anise
½ pint strong wine or brandy
1½ pounds raisins
3 cakes yeast

★ ★ ★ ★ ★

DIET PUMPKIN BREAD

From Farm Paper

1/3 cup cooking oil
1 tablespoon Sucaryl
3 eggs beaten
1 cup canned or cooked pumpkin
1 2/3 cup flour
1 teaspoon cinnamon
1 teaspoon soda

½ teaspoon nutmeg
¼ teaspoon baking powder
¼ teaspoon ginger
1/3 cup water
½ teaspoon salt
½ cup chopped nuts (optional)

Mix first 3 ingredients together then add remaining ingredients. Bake in greased, and floured 9 x 5 loaf pan. Bake in 350 degree oven for 40 – 50 minutes or until done. Turn out on wire rack to cool. Cool before slicing. (Freezes well.)

* * * * *

PUMPKIN BREAD

1 cup brown sugar, firmly packed
½ cup granulated sugar
1 cup cooked or canned pumpkin
½ cup salad oil
2 eggs, unbeaten
2 cups sifted all-purpose flour
1 teaspoon soda

½ teaspoon salt
½ teaspoon nutmeg
½ teaspoon cinnamon
¼ teaspoon ginger
1 cup raisins
½ cup chopped nuts
¼ cup water

Combine sugars, pumpkin, oil and eggs; beat until well blended. Sift together flour, soda, salt, and spices; add and mix well. Stir in raisins, nuts and water. Spoon into well oiled 9 x 5 x 3 loaf pan. Bake at 350 degrees for 65 – 75 minutes, or until done when tested. Turn out on rack to cool.

* * * * *

PUMPKIN BREAD

From WI State Journal – Dec 10, 1967

2/3 cup shortening
2 2/3 cups sugar
4 eggs
1 can (1 pound) pumpkin
2/3 cup water
3 1/3 cups all purpose flour
2 teaspoons soda

2½ teaspoons salt
½ teaspoon baking powder
1 teaspoon cinnamon
1 teaspoon cloves
2/3 cup coarsely chopped nuts
2/3 cup raisins

Heat oven to moderate (350 degrees) Grease two loaf pans, 9 x 5 x 3. Cream shortening and sugar thoroughly. Add eggs, pumpkin, and water. Blend in dry ingredients except nuts and raisins. Stir in nuts and raisins. Bake in prepared pans 65 – 75 minutes or until wooden pick inserted in center comes out clean.

* * * * *

PUMPKIN BREAD

From Farm Paper (Jean)

¾ cup shortening
2 2/3 cups sugar
2 cups pumpkin
4 eggs, well beaten
1 cup nuts, chopped

3½ cups flour
1 teaspoon cinnamon
½ teaspoon cloves
½ teaspoon salt
½ teaspoon baking powder

Combine and set aside to cool:
½ cup cut up dates
2/3 cup hot water
2 teaspoon baking soda

Combine all ingredients. Fold in nuts. Pour into greased and floured 9 x 5 loaf pans. Bake at 325 degrees for one hour. Makes 2 loafs. When done, turn out on cooling rack. Cool before slicing.

* * * * *

PUMPKIN CRANBERRY NUT BREAD

3½ cups flour
2 teaspoons ground cinnamon
1 teaspoon salt
1 teaspoon baking soda
½ teaspoon baking powder
2 teaspoons grated orange rind
¾ cup butter or margarine, softened

2 cups sugar
3 eggs
1 can (16 oz) solid pack pumpkin
1 cup chopped walnuts
1 cup chopped cranberries
Icing, walnuts, cranberry for garnish
    (optional)

Preheat oven to 350 degrees. Combine dry ingredients; set aside. Cream butter and sugar together. Add eggs one at a time, mixing after each addition. Alternate additions of pumpkin and dry ingredients. Stir in nuts and cranberries. Pour batter into two lightly greased 8 ½ x 4 ½ x 2 ½ inch loaf pans. Bake 60 – 65 minutes or until bread tests done. If desired, drizzle with icing (mix just enough cream or milk into powdered sugar to make a slightly runny consistency); garnish with walnut halves and cranberry. Yield: two loaves.

* * * * *

PUMPKIN RAISIN NUT BREAD

From: Lavon Brandt

3½ cups flour
½ teaspoon baking powder
2 teaspoons soda
1½ teaspoon cinnamon
1 teaspoon nutmeg
1 teaspoon cloves

3 cups sugar
1 cup water
4 eggs
2 cups pumpkin
½ cup nuts

Mix all ingredients together in order given. Pour into pans. Bake for 1 hour and 15 minutes at 350 degrees.

* * * * *

REFRIGERATOR ROLLS

2 (1 oz) cakes compressed yeast or 3
    packages dry yeast
1 cup lukewarm water
1 cup boiling water
1/3 cup lard or Crisco

½ cup butter
¾ cup sugar
1½ teaspoon salt
2 eggs beaten
6 – 8 cups flour

Soften yeast in lukewarm water.
Combine boiling water, lard, butter, sugar and salt. Stir until dissolved. Cool to lukewarm.
Add dissolved yeast and beaten eggs.
Mix in flour to make stiff dough. Refrigerate until ready to use. *(Granny used hers right away.)*
Knead until dough is smooth as it is used.
Make into rolls. Grease the tops. Let double in bulk – about 2 hours. Bake in 425 degree oven for 15 – 20 minutes.

Cinnamon Rolls

Roll dough out. Spread with melted butter. Then sprinkle with sugar and cinnamon. Roll up, cut in 2 inch slices. Put in greased pan. Rise, Bake. Turn out of pan, cool and frost.

* * * * *

ZUCCHINI BREAD

1 cup oil
1 1/3 cup sugar
3 cups flour
2 cups grated zucchini with seeds and skin
  removed
3 eggs

½ cup nuts
2 teaspoons vanilla
1 teaspoon baking soda
½ teaspoon baking powder
1 teaspoon salt
3 teaspoons cinnamon

* * * * *

ZUCCHINI BREAD

From Shopping News

Beat 3 eggs until light and foamy. Add 1 cup oil, 1½ - 2 cups sugar, 3 teaspoons vanilla, and 2 cups grated zucchini. Mix lightly, but well. Add 3 cups sifted flour, 1 teaspoon salt, 1 teaspoon soda, 3 teaspoons cinnamon and ½ teaspoon baking powder to batter and mix well. Chopped nuts, raisins, or currants are optional. Pour into two 9 x 5 x 3 inch greased loaf pans and bake for 45 minutes to 1 hour at 350 degrees.

* * * * *

ZUCCHINI BREAD

1 cup oil
1 1/3 cups sugar
3 cups flour
2 cups grated zucchini w/seeds and skin
  removed
3 eggs

½ cup nuts
2 teaspoons vanilla
1 teaspoon baking soda
½ teaspoon baking powder
1 teaspoon salt
3 teaspoon cinnamon

Sift together dry ingredients. Mix oil and sugar and add to dry ingredients. Add rest of ingredients. Bake in two small loaf pans at 350 degrees for 1 hour.

* * * * *

Doughnuts & Breakfast Items

APPLE COFFEE CAKE

From Wisconsin Agriculturist Oct 1974

½ cup light brown sugar
2 tablespoons flour
2 tablespoons butter
1 – 2 teaspoons cinnamon, as desired
½ - ¾ cup sugar, as desired
¼ cup shortening

1 egg
½ cup milk
1½ cup unsifted flour
2 teaspoons baking powder
½ teaspoon salt
2 cups thinly sliced apples

Blend brown sugar, 2 tablespoon flour, butter and cinnamon. In another bowl, combine sugar, shortening and eggs. Beat thoroughly. Stir in milk. Mix 1½ cup flour, baking powder and salt thoroughly. Stir into egg mixture just until smooth. Spread half the batter in a greased 9 inch square pan. Cover with half the apples. Top with half the brown sugar mixture. Repeat. Bake at 375 degrees for 45 – 50 minutes or until cake is set. If preferred, put all the batter in the pan at once. Arrange apples on top and sprinkle with brown sugar mixture. Makes 9 servings.

* * * * *

APPLE SPICE MUFFINS

From Wisconsin Agricultural Magazine Oct 1974

¾ cup milk
1 egg, beaten
¼ cup melted fat
2 cups unsifted flour
½ cup sugar

1 tablespoon baking powder
½ teaspoon salt
1 teaspoon cinnamon
1 cup finely chopped apples
¼ cup raisins

Add milk to egg; stir in fat. Mix dry ingredients thoroughly. Stir in apples and raisins. Add liquid mixture and stir just until most of dry ingredients are moistened. Do not over mix. Batter should be lumpy. Fill greased muffin tins 2/3 full. Bake at 400 degrees 20 – 25 minutes until golden brown. Makes 12 muffins.

* * * * *

BAKED BREAKFAST BROWN RICE

From Mrs. D.J. Hunter Corona, CA – Prevention Magazine

Full of nutrients and a nice change in the morning menu.

2 cups cooked brown rice
1 cup raisins
1½ cups soymilk

Mix all ingredients. Pour into deep casserole dish. Cover. Bake for 45 minutes at 325 degrees. Serve hot with honey and additional soy milk. This dish may be prepared in the evening and refrigerated overnight. Slip the casserole into the oven upon arising and breakfast is ready when the family is.

* * * * *

BUTTERMILK DOUGHNUTS

From Wisconsin College of Agriculture

1 egg
1 cup sugar
1 cup buttermilk
1½ tablespoons melted lard
4 cups flour

1¾ teaspoon soda
1¾ teaspoon cream of tartar
1½ teaspoon salt
1 teaspoon grated nutmeg

Beat egg until light, and add sugar, buttermilk and soda mixed. Then add lard. Mix and sift flour with remaining ingredients and add to first mixture. Toss on a floured cloth, knead slightly, pat and roll to ¼ inch thickness. Shape with a doughnut cutter, first dipped in flour. Fry in deep fat. Take up on skewer and drain on brown paper.

* * * * *

COFFEE CAKE

From Chris

Cream until light and fluffy:
½ cup butter
1¼ cup sugar
2 eggs

Sift:
2 cups flour
½ teaspoon soda
1½ teaspoon baking powder

Blend in:
1 cup sour cream

Add to creamed mixture with
1 teaspoon vanilla

Blend well. Grease and flour tube pan. Spoon half the batter in.
Combine and then sprinkle in:
¾ cup nuts (walnuts)
1 teaspoon cinnamon
2 tablespoons sugar

Top with remaining batter. Place in cold oven at 350 degrees about 50 minutes (check). Let stand in pan 15 – 20 minutes. Flavor improves with age.

* * * * *

CREAM CHEESE COFFEE CAKE

From Mrs. Rose Bloom

1 stick butter (1/4 lb)
1 (8-oz) package cream cheese
1¼ cups white sugar
2 eggs

1 teaspoon baking powder
½ teaspoon salt
2 cups flour
¾ cup milk

Beat at medium speed for five minutes until light and fluffy. Spread half of batter in 9 x 12 pan, greased and floured. Sprinkle with half of topping mixture; spread remainder of batter in pan. Sprinkle on the rest of the topping. Bake coffee cake at 350 degrees for 40 – 45 minutes.

Topping

½ cup brown sugar
½ cup flour
¼ cup butter
1 teaspoon cinnamon

Mix all together until crumbly.

* * * * *

DATE OATMEAL MUFFINS

Good

2 cups buttermilk
2 cups rolled oats
1 cup firmly packed brown sugar
2 eggs, beaten
½ cup salad oil

2 cups sifted flour
1 teaspoon salt
4 teaspoons baking powder
1 teaspoon baking soda
1 pound chopped dates

Pour buttermilk over oats and sugar, which have been mixed. Add eggs and oil. Sift dry ingredients together. Add to oat mixture and stir just to moisten. Fold in dates.

Fill greased muffin tins 2/3 full. Bake in moderate (375 degree) oven for 25 – 30 minutes.

Yield: 24 muffins.
NOTE: These freeze well.

* * * * *

★ DOUGHNUTS

From: Mrs. Rote

1+ cups sugar
2 tablespoons melted butter
3 eggs
½ teaspoon soda
¼ teaspoon salt

1 cup sour milk
½ teaspoon cinnamon
½ teaspoon nutmeg
4 cups flour
1+ teaspoon baking powder

* * * * *

★ DOUGHNUTS

From Granny Babler

Beat:
3 eggs

Add:
1+ cup sugar
2 tablespoons melted butter

Mix in:
1 cup sour milk (or buttermilk) – add ½ teaspoon baking soda

Mix together:
4 cups flour
½ teaspoon nutmeg
1+ teaspoon baking powder
¼ teaspoon salt

Mix all together, roll out, cut out and fry in hot Crisco oil.

* * * * *

DOUGHNUTS

From Mrs. Ladwig

Good

1 cup cold mashed potatoes
1 cup sugar
1 tablespoon butter
1 teaspoon salt
1 teaspoon nutmeg

1 teaspoon vanilla
1 cup sweet milk (you can use sour milk)
3 eggs
4 level cups flour
4 teaspoons baking powder

Flour your baking board and take 1/3 of the dough and pat it out until it is ½ inch thick. Then cut 4 inch strips and tie them into a knot. In a heavy skillet, melt a combination lard and Crisco. Heat that until a drop of dough turns brown when dropped in. Put doughnuts into the hot shortening and they will sink. When they come to the top, turn them watch until they are brown.

Take them out and roll in a mixture of:
1 cup sugar
1 teaspoon cinnamon
½ cup powdered sugar

* * * * *

DOUGHNUTS

From Mother

1 cup sugar
1 cup buttermilk
1½ tablespoon lard
4 cups flour

½ teaspoon salt
1¾ teaspoon soda
1¾ teaspoon cream of tartar
1 teaspoon nutmeg

* * * * *

RAISED DOUGHNUTS

From Ruth Grossman

1½ cup scalded milk
1/3 cup butter
¼ cup sugar
2 yeast cakes in cup with 1 tablespoon
    sugar in ¼ cup warm water. (Let
    stand 5 minutes)

2 eggs beaten
5 cups flour
lemon flavor
1 teaspoon salt

Mix well. Let rise, then roll out and cut. Let rise again – double. Fry in hot grease.

* * * * *

RAISED DOUGHNUTS

From Mrs. Arthur Hartwig

1 cup scalded milk, cooled
2 packages dry yeast
½ cup sugar
1 teaspoon salt
2 eggs, well beaten

4½ - 4¾ cups sifted flour
½ cup melted butter, cooled
½ teaspoon nutmeg, or 1 teaspoon grated
    lemon rind, for flavor

Add yeast to milk. Add sugar and salt and let stand 5 minutes. Add eggs and ½ of the flour. Beat until smooth. Add butter and the rest of flour to make very soft dough.

Knead lightly on well-floured board until smooth and elastic. Let rise in greased bowl until double in bulk. Punch down and let rise again. Punch again and let stand 10 minutes.

Roll out to 1/3 inch thickness and cut with doughnut cutter. Let rise 30 minutes and drop top side down in hot fat (365 degrees.) Fry until brown; drain. May be sugared or glazed.

* * * * *

GOLDEN OATMEAL MUFFINS WITH BUTTER-CRUNCH TOPPING

From Jane Wells

1 cup sifted flour
¼ cup sugar
1 tablespoon baking powder
½ teaspoon salt

1 cup uncooked oatmeal
3 tablespoons melted butter
1 egg, beaten
1 cup milk

Sift together dry ingredients; stir in oats. Add butter, egg and milk, stirring until just moistened. Fill greased muffin cups 2/3 full. Sprinkle butter-crunch topping over unbaked muffins. Bake 425 dogrooc for 12 – 15 minutes. Makes 1 dozen.

Butter-Crunch Topping

1/3 cup brown sugar
2 tablespoons flour
2 teaspoons cinnamon
1 tablespoon melted butter

Combine ingredients and sprinkle over unbaked muffins.

* * * * *

PEANUT BUTTER-HONEY MUFFINS

1 beaten egg
1/3 cup honey
1/3 cup peanut butter
¼ cup salad oil
¾ cup milk

1 cup flour
1½ teaspoons baking powder
½ teaspoon salt
¼ teaspoon mace
1 cup uncooked Ralston cereal

Heat oven to hot (400 degrees). Combine egg, peanut butter, honey, salad oil and milk. Add to dry ingredients; stir only until dry ingredients are moistened. Bake in greased muffin pans filled 2/3 full 20 – 25 minutes or until brown. Yield: 12 muffins.

* * * * *

SOUR MILK WAFFLES

From Mrs. Martin Dickson

1¼ cup flour
½ teaspoon soda
½ teaspoon salt
1 tablespoon sugar

2 eggs
1 cup sour milk
¼ cup melted butter

Beat egg yolks, add milk and butter. Stir in dry ingredients. Fold in beaten egg whites. Makes four large waffles.

* * * * *

ZUCCHINI PANCAKES

From Nona Manke
La Crescenta, CA – Prevention

Zucchini is a good source of vitamin A, also supplies vitamin C, protein and minerals. The soy flour boosts the protein value of this dish. There are many ways to enjoy zucchini. This one is a particular favorite with children. Serve unsweetened applesauce or honey-sweetened applesauce as an accompaniment.

3 zucchini squash
1 egg
3 tablespoons soy flour

½ onion chopped (if desired)
½ teaspoon sea salt or kelp
¼ cup cold-pressed oil

Grate zucchini. Add beaten egg, soy flour, chopped onion and salt. Mix together. Heat oil in skillet. Form small pancakes and brown slightly on both sides.

* * * * *

Salads

APPLE SLICES

From: Barb Hartwig

2½ cups flour
1 tablespoon sugar
1 teaspoon salt
1 cup lard

Mix together like pie crust.

1 egg (separated). Put egg yolk in cup, add milk to make 2/3 cup.

Add to above mixture. Roll out ½ of the dough to fit jelly roll pan.
Cover crust with 2/3 cup cornflakes. Add 5 cups of sliced apples (peeled)
Mix 1½ cups of sugar with 1 teaspoon cinnamon. Sprinkle over the apples.
Roll out the other half of the crust. Put over the apples. Beat egg whites fairly stiff. Spread on top. Bake in 400 degree oven for 40 minutes.
While hot, drizzle with frosting:

1 cup confectioner's sugar
Little milk
Lemon flavoring

* * * * *

CHERRY SALAD

From Louise Rundhaug

½ cup 'red hot' cinnamon candies
1 cup water
1 small box cherry gelatin
1½ cup applesauce

1 (8 oz) package cream cheese
½ cup chopped nuts
½ cup chopped celery
½ cup salad dressing

Dissolve cinnamon candies in water. Simmer for a short time to dissolve completely. Add gelatin and applesauce. Pour half of this in ring mold. Chill to set. Mix rest of ingredients and spread over gelatin layer. Then pour on remaining gelatin. Chill until set.

* * * * *

COCKTAIL

Slice bananas
Slice oranges
Slice apples
Slice pineapples
Then chop walnut meats on top of all, and serve.

* * * * *

FANCY FRUIT SALAD – CHERRY SALAD SUPREME

From Better Homes & Gardens

1 (3 oz) package raspberry flavored gelatin
1 (21 oz) can cherry pie filling
1 (3 oz) package lemon gelatin
1 (3 oz) package cream cheese

1/3 cup mayonnaise or salad dressing
1 (8 ¾ oz) can crushed pineapple
½ cup whipping cream
1 cup tiny marshmallows

Dissolve raspberry gelatin in 1 cup boiling water; stir in pie filling. Pour into 9 x 9 x 2 baking dish and chill till partially set.

Dissolve lemon gelatin in 1 cup boiling water. Beat together cream cheese and mayonnaise. Gradually add lemon gelatin. Stir in undrained pineapple. Whip ½ cup whipping cream. Fold into lemon mixture with 1 cup tiny marshmallows. Spread atop cherry layer. Top with 2 tablespoons chopped nuts. Chill till set. Makes 12 servings.

* * * * *

FESTIVE STRAWBERRY SALAD

2 (3 oz) packages strawberry gelatin
1½ cup boiling water
16-oz (No. 2 can) crushed pineapple

½ cup pecans
1 (16 oz) package frozen strawberries
1 cup sour cream

Dissolve gelatin in boiling water; add frozen berries mixing gently until slightly congealed. Add pineapple and pecans. Put half of mixture into oiled mold and chill until firm. Add sour cream to remainder and pour carefully over congealed mixture. Chill until firm. Unmold. Serves 10-12.

* * * * *

FRUIT SALAD

2 tablespoons gelatin
1½ cups boiling water
¼ cup cold water
¼ cup lemon juice
2 tablespoons sugar

1 cup grapes
1 banana
1 apple
2 oranges
¼ cup chopped nutmeats

Soak gelatin in cold water and dissolve in hot water. Add sugar. Cut grapes in half and remove seeds. Slice banana, peel and chop the apple. Section the oranges. When liquid mixture begins to thicken, add fruit and nuts. Mold and chill. Serve with mayonnaise.

* * * * *

GRAPE CONFETTI SALAD

1 package (6 oz) lemon flavored gelatin
2 cups boiling water
1 1/3 cups cold water
¼ cup cider vinegar
½ teaspoon salt
2 cups halved and seeded fresh grapes

2/3 cup finely shredded cabbage
2/3 cup thinly sliced celery
½ cup shredded carrot
Salad greens
Ginger Dressing

In mixing bowl, dissolve gelatin in boiling water. Cool. Stir in cold water, vinegar and salt into the gelatin. Chill mixture until gelatin is syrupy. Spoon about ½ cup mixture into a 6 cup mold and arrange a few grape halves in mold. Chill until set. Mix remaining grapes, cabbage, celery and carrot into the remaining gelatin. Pour into mold over decorative layer. Chill until firm. Unmold salad on serving dish. Garnish with salad greens and serve with Ginger Dressing.

Ginger Dressing:

½ cup mayonnaise
½ cup dairy sour cream

½ teaspoon grated lemon peel
1 teaspoon ground ginger

In small bowl, thoroughly combine mayonnaise, sour cream, lemon peel and ginger.

Makes 8 servings.

* * * * *

GRAPES WITH SOUR CREAM

2½ cups seedless grapes
2/3 cup dairy sour cream
1 teaspoon slivered orange peel

2 tablespoons orange juice
¼ cup light brown sugar

Combine grapes with sour cream, orange peel and juice. Chill for at least one hour to allow flavors to blend. Sprinkle with brown sugar before serving.

* * * * *

LUSCIOUS SALAD

From Boots

1 pint soured cream
1 can (No 2 ½) sliced pineapple
10 oz can moist coconut
½ bag marshmallows cut in small pieces

Drain pineapple and cut into small pieces. Mix with other ingredients and put in covered bowl in refrigerator. Can be prepared in evening or early morning. Serve with a cherry on top.

* * * * *

MANDARIN ORANGE SALAD

Mrs. Emil Schiesser, Winslow

Drain and combine:
1 (8 oz) can pineapple tidbits
1 (8 oz) can fruit cocktail
1 (8 oz) can mandarin oranges

Add:
1 cup cottage cheese
1 carton cultured sour cream
1 cup miniature marshmallows

Garnish with maraschino cherries. Chill for several hours before serving.

* * * * *

OVERNIGHT SALAD AND DRESSING

From Mrs. Leo Gerber

Dressing:

4 tablespoons sugar
4 tablespoons vinegar

2 tablespoons butter
2 eggs

Cook mixture in double boiler until it coats the spoon.
Cool then add:
1 cup cream – whipped
2 cups miniature marshmallows
1 can mandarin oranges

1 cup pineapple tidbits
2 cups white grapes or white cherries

Chill overnight before serving.

* * * * *

PARTY DREAM SALAD

1 package (8 oz) cream cheese, softened
¼ cup dairy sour cream
2 tablespoons confectioners' sugar
1 tablespoon lemon juice
½ teaspoon salt

½ cup diced orange sections
½ cup halved maraschino cherries
½ cup coarsely chopped pecans
2 cups diced bananas
2 cups whipping cream

In a small mixing bowl, beat together cream cheese, sour cream, confectioners sugar, lemon juice and salt until light and fluffy. Fold in oranges, cherries, pecans, bananas and whipped cream. Turn into mold, chill until firm. Unmold onto serving plate. Garnish with maraschino cherries.

* * * * *

PATIO FRUIT SALAD

4 bananas cut into large chunks
2 oranges, peeled and sliced
½ fresh pineapple, cut into spears (or drained canned pineapple)
½ cantaloupe, sliced

1 cup blueberries
1 cup sliced strawberries
¼ small watermelon, cut into wedges
Fruit Salad Dressing

Arrange fruit and small bowl of dressing on platter.
Yield: 6 – 8 servings.

Fruit Salad Dressing

1/3 cup dairy sour cream
1/3 cup mayonnaise
2 ripe bananas, peeled and mashed
Combine ingredients.

1 tablespoon honey
2 tablespoons finely chopped toasted almonds

* * * * *

PINEAPPLE MARSHMALLOW SALAD

From Donna Siedschlag

2 cups colored miniature marshmallows
1 package (8 oz) cream cheese, have at room temperature

1 pkg dream whip
1 small can crushed pineapple, drained
½ cup coconut

Whip cream according to directions on the package. Add cream cheese and beat until well mixed. Add marshmallows, pineapple and coconut. Refrigerate several hours.

* * * * *

PINEAPPLE SALAD

From Linda

Juice from 1 (20 oz) can of pineapple (chunks, tidbits, etc)

Add (and mix together):
2 tablespoons flour
3 tablespoons sugar
2 eggs, well beaten

Cook until thickened. When cool add pineapple, bananas, marshmallows.

* * * * *

RASPBERRY SUPREME

From Ella E. Copelan, Sweet Home, Ore (Prevention)

Serve a dessert like this and who needs cake?

1 cup cooked brown rice (hot)
1 cup nut milk

2 eggs
1 tablespoon honey

Mix together and cook on low heat until thick, stirring constantly. Add 1 cup fresh or frozen berries. Serve hot or cold.

* * * * *

SALAD

From Mrs. Louise Kaderly

1 small can mandarin oranges, drained
1 small can crushed pineapple, drained
½ cup coconut

2 cups small marshmallows
1 small package sour cream
3 tablespoons powdered sugar

Combine sour cream and powdered sugar and mix with rest of ingredients.

(Optional – fruit cocktail instead of oranges.)

* * * * *

TWENTY FOUR HOUR SALAD

From Boots

1 bag marshmallows
1 small can white cherries
1 large (or 2 med) can tidbit pineapple
Cut marshmallows and drain fruit (save juice).

Boil together:
4 egg yolks
1 cup fruit juice

4 teaspoons cornstarch
1 teaspoon salt

While hot add juice and rind of one lemon. When cool add to fruit and marshmallows. Put in refrigerator. When ready to serve add 1 pint whipping cream (whipped).

* * * * *

YUM-YUM SALAD

From Boots

1 pkg lemon Jell-O
1 pkg lime Jell-O
2 cups hot water
1 can pet milk

1 pkg cottage cheese
1 cup mayonnaise
1 flat can crushed pineapple
1 cup nut meats

Mix all ingredients together. Refrigerate and serve.

* * * * *

Jell-O

CRANBERRY JELLO SALAD

Grind up:
2 cups cranberries
1 orange

Add:
1 cup sugar

Let stand for 2 hours

Mix:
1 pkg strawberry Jell-O
1 cup boiling water
(NOTE: add more gelatin or less water)

½ cup marshmallows cut up
½ cup apples cut up
½ cup celery, cut up
½ cup crushed pineapple
few nutmeats

* * * * *

HELEN'S FAVORITE SHERBET SALAD

2 packages (3 oz each) lime-flavored
    gelatin
1 cup boiling water

1 pint lime sherbet
1 can (11 oz) mandarin oranges, drained
1 cup heavy cream, whipped

Dissolve gelatin in boiling water. Add sherbet and mix well. When partially set, fold in oranges and whipped cream. Pour into well-oiled mold (1½ quarts). Chill.

* * * * *

★ LIME AND COTTAGE CHEESE SALAD

From Mr. Ralph Seidschlag

1 package lime Jell-O
small can crushed pineapple
12 diced marshmallows

1 cup cottage cheese
½ cup pecans
½ pint whipping cream, whipped

Put pineapple juice in cup and add water to make two cups. Place in a saucepan with Jell-O and boil two minutes. Cool until set. Fold in rest of ingredients, folding in cream last.

* * * * *

GELATIN CHERRY CREAM MOLD

From: Mrs. Martha Silbuagh – Santa Cruz, CA

Here's a festive gelatin dessert make without sugar.

2 envelopes or 2 tablespoons gelatin
2 cups yogurt
1½ cup cherries, raw, pitted

½ teaspoon vanilla extract
1 sprig mint
2 tablespoons honey

Soften gelatin in ½ cup of water. In blender, mix gelatin and ¾ cup cherries. Add yogurt, vanilla extract, honey, and sprig of mint; blend well. Stir in remaining cherries. Turn into mold and chill until set.

Variation: Cranberries or other berries in season may be used in place of cherries. Nuts or sunflower seeds may be added.

* * * * *

GLAZED PEACH CRÈME

2 pkg (3 oz) peach flavor gelatin
2 cups boiling water
¾ cup cold water
1 pint vanilla ice cream
1 can (8¾ oz) sliced peaches or one fresh peach peeled and sliced.

Dissolve one pkg gelatin in 1 cup boiling water. Add cold water. Chill until slightly thickened (gelatin will have the consistency of unbeaten egg whites).

Dissolve second package gelatin in remaining boiling water. Add ice cream and stir until melted and smooth. Pour into serving bowl. Chill about 1 hour until set, but not firm.

Arrange canned or fresh peach slices on gelatin-ice cream mixture.

Top with clear gelatin. Garnish with prepared Dream Whip whipped topping if desired. Makes 5 cups or 10 servings.

* * * * *

JELLIED WALDORF SALAD

1 package (3 oz) orange-flavored gelatin
dash salt
1 cup boiling water
¾ cup cold water

1 tablespoon lemon juice
¾ cup diced unpeeled apple
¼ cup chopped celery
¼ cup chopped walnuts

Dissolve gelatin and salt in boiling water. Add cold water and lemon juice. Chill until slightly thickened. Stir in remaining ingredients. Spoon into a greased 4 cup mold. Chill.

* * * * *

ORANGAE SALAD

From Paper: Mrs. Ray Dye - Monroe

For first layer: Dissolve 1 pkg orange Jell-O (3 oz) in 1 cup boiling water.

Then add 2 cups vanilla ice cream. Stir until dissolved.

Put into a 7 x 11 inch loaf pan. Refrigerate until firm.

For second layer: Dissolve 1 pkg orange Jell-O in 1½ cups boiling liquid (water and fruit juice). Dissolve and let set until it starts to congeal.

Add 1 can mandarin orange segments (drained). Put over the first layer. Refrigerate again. To serve, cut into squares. Serves 8.

* * * * *

ORANGE SALAD

Editor's Note: This is the Orange Salad recipe Granny gave me.
2 pkgs orange gelatin
2 cups hot water
1 cup orange juice
1 pint orange sherbet
1 cup heavy cream (Granny uses Cool Whip)
1 can mandarin oranges, drained

Dissolve gelatin in 2 cups hot water. Add orange juice and chill until partially set. Whip mixture until light and fluffy; add sherbet and mix well. (Granny beats this too). Fold in whipped cream and oranges. Pour into mold and chill until firm. Garnish with additional orange sections and maraschino cherries.

* * * * *

SUMMER COOL SALAD

Use 10 cup mold, oiled
Makes 10-12 servings

18 large marshmallows
1 cup milk
1 pkg (6 oz) lemon flavored gelatin
1 can (No. 2) crushed pineapple, undrained
1 cup grated carrot

1 cup chopped celery
1 cup creamed, small curd cottage cheese
½ cup dairy sour cream
1 cup whipping cream, whipped
½ cup chopped nuts

Melt marshmallows in milk in top of double boiler. Pour the hot mixture over gelatin. Stir until dissolved. Cool. Add pineapple, carrots, celery, cottage cheese and sour cream. Chill this until jellied, and then fold in the whipped cream and nuts. Pour in mold and refrigerate.

* * * * *

26

SUNRISE SALAD

From S. H. Ray

Dissolve 1 package lemon gelatin in 1 cup boiling water. Let cool and thicken until quivery but not hard. Add ½ cup drained, crushed pineapple, 1/3 cup orange juice, ½ cup grated carrots, ¼ cup chopped green pepper, 1 cup finely chopped cabbage, ¼ teaspoon salt, ¼ teaspoon paprika mixed with ½ cup cottage cheese. Chill in mold until stiff. Serve on finely shredded cabbage or lettuce with mayonnaise.

* * * * *

WHIPPED CREAM WALNUT MOLD

1 package lemon-flavored gelatin
1 cup hot water
1 cup apricot juice
1 cup cottage cheese

1 cup whipping cream, whipped
½ cup chopped walnut meats
½ cup maraschino cherries, quartered
1 cup sliced apricots

Dissolve gelatin in hot water. Add apricot juice. Chill until partially set. Fold in cottage cheese and whipped cream, walnut meats, cherries and apricots. Pour into oiled mold and chill until firm. Makes 8 servings.

* * * * *

Misc Salads

GAZPACHO ASPIC

Serves 6

2 tablespoons unflavored gelatin
1 cup beef stock
¼ cup lemon juice
2¼ cups tomato juice
1 large green pepper, finely chopped

1 large sweet red pepper, finely chopped
2 medium size cucumbers, peeled, seeded
 and coarsely chopped
3 green onions, thinly sliced
2 tablespoons minced parsley

1. Lightly oil a 6 cup decorative mold and set it aside.
2. Sprinkle the gelatin over the stock in a small saucepan and allow to stand 5 minutes to soften. Place on medium heat. Stir gently until gelatin dissolves. Remove from heat and cool to room temperature. Transfer to a large mixing bowl. Stir in the lemon juice and tomato juice. Cover and chill until mixture is the consistency of unbeaten egg white. Stir occasionally.
3. Mix the remaining ingredients into the loosely set gelatin mixture. Turn into the mold. Cover and chill until set (about 6 hours).
4. Unmold before serving.

* * * * *

FAST RHUBARB SALAD

Bring to a boil, reduce
heat and simmer:
4 cups diced pie plant
1 cup water
¾ cup sugar
¼ teaspoon salt

Mix together and chill until
partially thickened:
2 (3 oz) packages of
strawberry Jell-O
1½ cup cold water
¼ cup lemon juice

Stir into Jell-O:
Cooled rhubarb
1 cup diced celery
2 (11-oz) cans mandarin
oranges (drained)

Spoon into a dish. After it has set, top with dairy sour cream and nutmeg.

* * * * *

GLORIFIED RICE

Editor's Note: This is the recipe Granny gave me.
Using Minute Rice – cook rice for 6 servings. (Use more water than they say, cook for 5 minutes. Let it set for 5 minutes, and then pour off any extra water.) Let this cool. Add 1 small can of crushed pineapple, maraschino cherries. Sprinkle rice with ½ cup sugar (or to taste.) If desired, you can add colored marshmallows and drained mandarin oranges. Stir in whipped cream a couple hours before serving. You can always add a little more whipped cream if necessary.

Whipped Cream – 2½ pints of whipping cream. Shake before whipping. Add powdered sugar to obtain the desired sweetness.

* * * * *

SOUFFLE SALAD

Basic recipe:

1 pkg lemon or lime Jell-O   ¼ teaspoon salt
1 cup hot water   dash of pepper
½ cup cold water   1 – 2 ½ cups vegetables, fruits, meats,
1 – 2 tablespoons vinegar or lemon juice   poultry, fish, cheese or eggs
½ cup mayonnaise

1. Dissolve Jell-O in hot water. Add the cold water, vinegar, mayonnaise, salt and pepper. Blend well with a rotary beater. Then pour into refrigerator freezing tray.
2. Quick-chill in freezing unit (without changing control) 15 – 20 minutes, or until firm about 1 inch from edge but soft in center. Turn mixture into bowl. Whip with rotary beater until fluffy.

   Those are the easy basic steps.... Here's where you own imagination takes over......

3. Fold in 1 – 2 ½ cups vegetables, fruits, fish, poultry, meat, cheese or eggs. Pour into 1 quart mold or individual molds. Chill until firm in the refrigerator 30 – 60 minutes. Unmold and garnish with salad greens. Serve with additional mayonnaise, if desired. Makes 4 – 6 servings.

Tuna Fish Soufflé Salad:

Make the basic soufflé salad using lemon Jell-O. Fold in 1 can (7 oz) tuna fish, flaked and drained, 1 cup diced celery, ¼ cup chopped pimento and 1 tablespoon finely chopped onion.

Garden Vegetable Soufflé Salad:

Make the basic soufflé salad using lemon Jell-O. Fold in 1/3 cup each diced cauliflower, shredded carrots, sliced radishes, diced celery and chopped water cress, spinach, endive, romaine or escarole, 2 tablespoons diced green pepper and 1 tablespoon finely chopped onion. Serve with crisp greens.

Cole Slaw Soufflé Salad:

Make the basic soufflé salad. Fold in 2 cups finely chopped cabbage, 2 tablespoons chopped green pepper, 1 tablespoon finely chopped onion, and ¼ teaspoon celery seed.

NOTE: When making vegetable and meat salads, add ½ - 1 tablespoon of finely chopped onion to the basic recipe, if desired. When making fruit salads, omit the pepper.

* * * * *

TART RHUBARB SALAD

4 cups diced fresh rhubarb
1 cup water
¾ cup sugar
¼ teaspoon salt
2 (3 oz) packages strawberry flavor gelatin

1¾ cup cold water
¼ cup lemon juice
1 cup diced celery
2 (11 oz) cans mandarin oranges, drained

Combine first four ingredients; bring to a boil. Reduce heat and simmer only until rhubarb loses crispness. Remove from heat. Add gelatin and stir until dissolved. Add cold water and lemon juice. Chill until partly thickened. Fold in celery and oranges; spoon into shallow 2 qt glass dish or into 8 individual molds. Chill until firm. Serve on crisp lettuce with sour cream; dust with nutmeg. Makes 8 servings.

* * * * *

Vegetable Salad

★ BEAN SALAD

1 can yellow beans
1 can green beans
1 can fancy red kidney beans – dark red

Heat separately and drain
Add green pepper and onion rings, diced celery and pimento

Dressing:

2/3 cup vinegar
¾ cup sugar
1 teaspoon salt
dash of pepper

Pour on top of above mixture
1/3 cup oil

Mix and pour over the beans. Let stand 8 – 12 hours.

* * * * *

CARROT CAPER

2 Envelopes Knox Unflavored Gelatin
2 cups orange juice
¼ teaspoon salt
1 cup Miracle Whip salad dressing

1 2/3 cups (13 ½ oz can) crushed
 pineapple
1½ cups grated carrot

Soften gelatin in 1 cup orange juice; stir over low heat until dissolved. Add remaining orange juice and salt. Gradually add gelatin to Miracle Whip, mixing until well blended. Chill until slightly thickened. Fold in pineapple and carrots. Pour into 1 ½ quart mold. Chill until firm. Unmold. Garnish with watercress and coin size slices of carrot. 8 servings.

* * * * *

CARROT SALAD

1 cup fresh carrots, chopped
1 cup celery, diced
½ green pepper, chopped
Salad Dressing
Put carrots through food chopper. Mix with celery and green peppers, or decorate with parsley, and serve on lettuce leaves with some dressing.

* * * * *

CELERY AND CABBAGE SALAD IN GREEN PEPPERS

Cut off stem end, remove seeds and veins of green peppers and fill with chopped celery and cabbage. Mix with boiled Mayonnaise.

* * * * *

CHINESE COLE SLAW

From Samuel Freeman Ocean Park, CA

For a delightful change – make this slaw with vitamin-rich, low-calorie Chinese cabbage.

Use Chinese cabbage instead of ordinary cabbage. And add nothing except a little vegetable salt and lemon juice. Be sure, however, that when you grate up the Chinese cabbage, it is cold, direct from the refrigerator. Once you eat Chinese coleslaw, you will not ever again, I'm sure, go back to the ordinary kind.

* * * * *

COLE SLAW

From Mary W. Jackson Horseheads, NY

The pineapple and nuts give this cole slaw extra nutrients and a delightful combination of flavors.

3 cups finely shredded cabbage
1 cup grated carrots
½ cup drained crushed pineapple (unsweetened)

½ cup chopped walnuts
1 tablespoon toasted sesame seeds

Combine above ingredients with dressing made of:

2/3 cups homemade mayonnaise

2 tablespoons apple cider vinegar
1 tablespoon honey

* * * * *

COOL COLESLAW

2 envelopes Knox Unflavored Gelatin
1½ cups cold water
1 teaspoon salt
2 tablespoons lemon juice
1 cup salad dressing

1 cup shredded cabbage
1 cup chopped celery
1 cup chopped peeled cucumber
½ cup chopped pimiento
3 tablespoons finely chopped onion

Soften Knox Gelatin in 1 cup cold water. Stir over low heat until dissolved. Stir in remaining water, salt and lemon juice. Gradually add gelatin to Salad Dressing, mixing until well blended. Chill until slightly thickened. Fold in remaining ingredients. Pour into 1½ quart mold and chill until firm. Unmold. Garnish with cherry tomatoes.

* * * * *

FRANK'S KRAUT SALAD

1 lb Frank's Quality Kraut
½ cup green pepper (cut fine)
2 cups celery (cut fine)

1 small onion (cut fine)
½ cup sugar
salt and pepper to taste

Drain Kraut. Mix all ingredients and let stand in refrigerator. Keeps well.

* * * * *

FROZEN SLAW

1 medium cabbage, shredded
1 teaspoon salt
3 ribs celery, chopped (optional)
½ green pepper, chopped
1 cup white vinegar

½ cup water
2 cups sugar
1 teaspoon celery seed
1 teaspoon mustard seed

Sprinkle salt over cabbage and let stand for 1 hour. Squeeze out fluid. Mix cabbage, celery, and green pepper. Mix remaining ingredients and bring to boil. Boil 1 minute. Cool. Pour over cabbage mixture and freeze. Thaw before serving.

* * * * *

HEARTY SPRING SALAD

1 package frozen Italian-style green beans,
    cooked and chilled
1 package frozen green limas, cooked and
    chilled
½ cup sliced radishes
2 medium onions, peeled and thinly sliced

3 red apples, unpeeled and cubed
1 cup cubed cheddar cheese
1 head romaine
½ pound sliced ham bologna
Herb dressing

Combine vegetables, apples and cheese. Toss with some of the herb dressing. Line salad bowls with romaine. Tear or cut remaining romaine into bite size pieces. Turn into salad bowl. Top with vegetable-apple mixture. Cut ham bologna slices in half, and arrange around rim of bowl. Serve remaining dressing separately. Makes 8 servings.

Herb dressing:

¼ teaspoon parsley flakes
¼ teaspoon dried mint
¼ teaspoon oregano
Combine all ingredients and mix well.

¼ cup grated carrot
1 cup bottled Italian dressing

* * * * *

RAW BEET GELATINE SALAD

From Marida Demler
Ramona, CA – Prevention

Add a piquant and colorful touch to your meal and supplies valuable enzymes because it's raw.

Combine in a blender with some pineapple
    juice:
1 carrot, raw
4 medium or 6 small fresh raw beets, cut
1 teaspoon undistilled apple cider vinegar
    (or lemon juice)

3 medium oranges
1 handful celery greens (2 ½ celery stalks)
1 handful china peas (edible pod peas)
2 tablespoons soaked seedless raisins with
    juice
some parsley

In a big bowl have ready the unflavored plain gelatin (I use 3 tablespoons to 2 cups of hot water.) Put all in bowl, refrigerate and eat the next day.

* * * * *

RAW SPINACH SALAD

From Mr. G. F. Wonff

3 cups fresh chopped spinach or frozen
    chopped spinach
2 hard boiled eggs, chopped fine
¼ cup celery, chopped fine
3 green onions, sliced thin

½ cup sour cream
½ cup mayonnaise
Salt and garlic salt to taste
Horseradish to taste (optional)
Lettuce leaves

Mix spinach, eggs, celery, and green onions together in bowl.

Combine sour cream, mayonnaise, salt, garlic salt and horseradish (if desired). Pour over spinach mixture and mix well. Refrigerate until ready to serve. Serve individually on lettuce leaves or pass in salad bowl.

Yield: Six to eight servings.

NOTE: If horseradish is not added to salad, it may be served on the side.

* * * * *

RAW VEGETABLE SALAD

1 small head cauliflower
3 carrots, coarsely shredded
3 large stalks celery, diagonally sliced
½ cup sliced pimento-stuffed olives
½ cup lightly packed celery leaves

¼ cup salad oil
¼ cup white vinegar
¼ cup water
1 teaspoon sugar
1 teaspoon seasoning salt

Into large bowl, break cauliflower into small flowerets. Add carrots, celery and olives. In covered blender – blend at high speed the celery leaves and the remaining ingredients until celery leaves are finely chopped. Pour over vegetables. Toss to mix well. Makes 8 servings.

★ RED KIDNEY BEAN SALAD

From Anna Falzone (Granny's sister)

1 can beans
3 hard boiled eggs
Sweet pickles
Salad Dressing

* * * * *

SAUERKRAUT SALAD

From Jean

1 large can sauerkraut (Franks)
3 sticks celery, cut up
1 green pepper, diced up
1 small onion, sliced

1 cup sugar
3 tablespoons vinegar
¼ cup oil

Drain and rinse kraut. Cut it up so it isn't so stringy. Add all other ingredients. Mix well and refrigerate.

* * * * *

SOUR CREAM COLE SLAW

6 servings

½ medium head cabbage, shredded (4 cups)
½ cup dairy sour cream
2 tablespoons sugar

2 tablespoons vinegar
½ teaspoon salt
dash of pepper

Combine all ingredients except cabbage. Then mix and pour over cabbage. Chill until ready to serve.

* * * * *

SOUR CREAM POTATO SALAD

5 cups cooked diced potatoes
½ cup finely diced cucumber
1 tablespoon finely diced onion
1 teaspoon celery seed
2 teaspoons salt

6 eggs, hard-cooked
¾ cup sour cream
¾ cup salad dressing
2 tablespoons vinegar
1 teaspoon prepared mustard

Toss together lightly the potatoes, cucumber, onion, and seasonings. Remove yolks from eggs. Chop egg whites and add to potato mixture. Press egg yolks through a sieve and combine with sour cream, salad dressings, vinegar, and mustard. Fold dressing mixture into potatoes. Chill well. Serves 8.

* * * * *

Meat Salads

HAM AND FRUIT SALAD

1 to 1 ¼ pound cooked smoked ham, cut
    in julienne strips 1/1/2 inches long
1 can (13 ¼ ounces) pineapple chunks

1 banana, peeled and sliced
1 avocado, peeled and sliced
½ medium-sized cantaloupe cut in balls.

Drain pineapple chunks, reserving juice. Pour juice over sliced banana and avocado; drain and reserve juice for dressing. Combine pineapple chunks, ham banana and avocado slices and cantaloupe balls and turn into lettuce lined bowl, cover and chill. Serve with Pineapple Dressing (6 servings.)

Pineapple Dressing

½ cup sugar
1 tablespoon flour
1 egg, slightly beaten

¾ cup pineapple juice
¼ cup lemon juice

Combine sugar and flour and stir into egg. Add juices, mixing well. Cook slowly, stirring constantly, until thickened. Cool before serving. Yield: 1½ cup.

* * * * *

HAM FRUIT SALAD

1 cup cooked cubed ham
½ cup diced orange
½ cup diced apple
¾ cup pineapple chunks
½ cup diced bananas
Dressing

Combine ingredients. Serve in lettuce cups with salad dressing. Try thinning your salad dressing with lemon juice and pineapple juice.

* * * * *

TUNA FISH SALAD

1 large can tuna fish
2 cups chopped celery
1 chopped green pepper
Boiled Salad Dressing

Remove skin and bones from fish. Break in ½ inch cubes, add celery and pepper. Arrange on salad plates on lettuce leaves and cover with boiled mayonnaise.
I have everything cold.

* * * * *

TURKEY SALAD FOR 25

From Paper Mrs. Jerry Wyttenbach, Argyle

12 Pound (disjointed) turkey cooked with 3 stalks celery, 3 carrots, 2 medium onions, and 3 tablespoons salt
2 (10 ½ oz) package frozen peas, cooked

1 quart salad dressing or mayonnaise
1 pint sour cream
1 cup sweet onion, diced
1 dozen hard-cooked eggs, diced
3 cups green grapes (fresh or canned)
Sugar to taste (2-4 tablespoons)
¾ gallon shoestring potatoes, added when serving.

Cook turkey with celery, carrots, onions, and salt until thicker turkey pieces are fork-tender. Drain (broth may be strained and used for soup). Cut turkey in cubes. Discard vegetables from broth.
Cook peas as directed on package. Cool and drain. Mix all ingredients except potatoes and chill well.

When ready to serve add the shoestring potatoes. (NOTE: Do not add potatoes to any portion being held to serve some time later . . .add when served).

* * * * *

TONGUE SALAD

From Mrs. Rote

Peas
Celery
Marshmallows
White cherries
Hard boiled eggs
Tongue

Mix with Salad Dressing

* * * * *

SALMON RICE SALAD

3 cups cooked rice
1 can [1 pound] salmon, drained and flaked
½ cup minced parsley
2 tablespoons minced chives or green
    onion tops

½ cup finely chopped celery
3 hard cooked eggs, chopped
Freshly ground black pepper
½ cup French dressing
Lemon slices

Combine rice, salmon, parsley, chives, celery and eggs. Sprinkle with pepper. Add French dressing and toss lightly. Garnish with lemon slices and chill until ready to serve. Makes six servings.

NOTE: Another equally delicious summer salad that doubles as a luscious sandwich filling.

* * * * *

SALMON EGG SALAD

1 can [7¾ oz] salmon
½ cup finely chopped celery
¼ cup chopped green onion
¼ cup chopped cucumber
2 hard cooked eggs, chopped

1/3 cup mayonnaise
½ teaspoon salt
1/8 teaspoon pepper
2 tablespoons minced parsley

Drain salmon, reserving liquid. Flake salmon. Combine flaked salmon, celery, onion, cucumber, and eggs. Combine mayonnaise with one tablespoon of the reserved salmon liquid, salt, pepper and parsley. Add to salmon mixture and mix lightly. Chill.

Use as salad or sandwich filling. Serves three to four.

* * * * *

Salad Dressings

CHIVE – LEMON MAYONNAISE DRESSING

From: Ruth Schwartz - New York, NY

It's so easy to make your own mayonnaise. Then you know it's fresh and free of additives. This one has extra zest and color because of chives.

1 large egg
¾ teaspoon sea salt
¾ teaspoon dried chives or 2 tablespoons chopped fresh chives

¼ teaspoon paprika
2 tablespoons fresh lemon juice
2 teaspoons apple cider vinegar
1 cup oil (cold-pressed)

Break the egg into the bowl of an electric blender. Add remaining ingredients except the oil and blend over low speed until smooth. Continue blending and add oil in a fine stream until oil is completely absorbed into the remaining ingredients and mixture is thick and smooth. Transfer to a screw top jar and keep in refrigerator.

* * * * *

SALAD DRESSING

6 tablespoons sugar
2 heaping teaspoons flour
½ teaspoon mustard
½ teaspoon salt

Mix these dry ingredients together with:
2 slightly beaten eggs
Add:
½ cup vinegar
¾ cup water

Boil till it thickens.
Add:
1 tablespoon butter and cool.
Mix with whip cream to the desired consistency.

* * * * *

SALAD DRESSING WITHOUT VINEGAR OR EGG

Good

1 tablespoon butter
1½ tablespoon flour
1 1/3 cup cream (sweet or sour)

¼ teaspoon salt
3 teaspoons sugar
3 tablespoons lemon juice

Melt butter. Add flour and stir till well blended. Add 2/3 cup of cream, stir till it boils and is smooth. Add salt, sugar and lemon juice. Turn into a double boiler and boil ten minutes stirring constantly.
When cold add 2/3 cup cream and stir till smooth. If the dressing is to be used on top of salad – whip the last 2/3 cup of cream stiff before adding to the mixture.

* * * * *

SWEET/SOUR DRESSING

Editor's Note: Granny gave me this recipe.
Dissolve:
1 cup sugar
1 cup vinegar
½ cup salad oil

Pour over vegetables – good for lettuce also.

* * * * *

Soups

BEAN SOUP

From Jean

3 + cups water (enough to cover whatever size ham bone you have.
Suggested: Ham Butt.)

Soak over night:
1 cup pea beans
1 cup white beans
1 cup mixed soup beans

parsley
celery
onion
little sugar
seasonings (whatever you like)

Worchester sauce
Soy Sauce
1 small can V8 juice
1 can stewed tomatoes

Cook in a slow cooker all day and at least part of the night.

* * * * *

CORN & BEAN SOUP

From R. Eugene Keesee

Corn and beans complement each other, making this a nicely balanced hearty soup.

Add 1 beef bone to a quart of water with the following ingredients:

1 small onion
1 celery stalk, chopped
 kernels from one ear of corn
½ cup pea beans, which have soaked
    overnight

½ teaspoon celery salt
parsley
pinoh of dill

Simmer till done.

* * * * *

LENTIL STEW

A meat substitute with a zesty flavor.

1 cup lentils
4 cups vegetable water
¼ - ½ teaspoon savory
1 tablespoon soy sauce

1 cup brown rice
1 small onion, chopped fine
½ cup carrots, diced
½ cup peas

Place lentils and 2½ cups water into 1½ quart casserole and simmer, covered, approximately 1 hour.

Add remaining water, rice, onion, savory and simmer, tightly covered approximately ½ hour.

Stir in carrots, a little more water if necessary, and simmer, covered for 15-30 minutes longer, or until carrots and rice are just about done.

Add soy sauce and peas and simmer until done.

Add kelp, bone meal or dolomite to increase mineral value.

Potatoes may be substituted for rice.

* * * * *

LENTIL SOUP

From Prevention

1 cup (untreated) lentils
1 onion (medium size)
½ cup celery leaves
½ cup parsley

2 tablespoons soy or oil
¼ teaspoon sweet basil
Kelp or sea salt to taste

Wash lentils and soak 2 hours. Chop onion, celery leaves and parsley very fine.
Add vegetables and soy or oil to lentils. Cook in water in which they were soaked. Simmer until tender. Add seasoning and simmer 5 minutes.

* * * * *

MEATS AND MAIN DISHES

ALL-IN-ONE MEAL

From Miss Rita Ball Lehigh Acres, FL

A nice combination of flavors, food values and fun in this meatball and 'secret' sprouts dish.

1 pound ground beef
1 cup cooked brown rice
2 tablespoons finely chopped onion
½ teaspoon thyme
1 pinch kelp
1 egg

½ pound Brussels sprouts
2 tablespoons cold-pressed oil
¼ cup water with 1 tablespoon dark honey (mixed)
½ cup tomato puree

Mix ground beef, rice, onion, kelp, thyme and egg. Shape a meat ball around each Brussels sprout. Brown meatballs on all sides in hot corn old in skillet. Pour off any excess fat. Pour on tomato puree and water-honey mixture. Simmer in covered skillet for 15 minutes.

Serve with mixed green salad.

* * * * *

BAKED HASH

1 pint chopped cooked meat
1 pint chopped row or cooked potatoes
1 cup gravy or water

Chopped onion
1 tablespoon melted butter
Salt to taste

Mix together, turn into mold and bake in a moderate oven one hour.

* * * * *

BARBECUED GROUND BEEF

1 pound ground beef
1 cup finely chopped onion
1 cup finely chopped green pepper
1 tablespoon sugar
2 tablespoons prepared mustard

1 tablespoon vinegar
1 teaspoon salt
1 cup catsup
½ teaspoon ground cloves
4-6 hamburger buns

Brown meat slowly until crumbly but not hard. Combine remaining ingredients and add to the meat. Cover and simmer about 30 minutes. Serve on split buns. 4-6 servings.

* * * * *

BAR-BE-QUE

1 lb corn beef loaf or bologna
2 large green peppers
1 large onion
1 bottle catsup

Chop corn beef (if bologna is used remove skin and put through food grinder). Put peppers and onion through grinder also. Put all in frying pan and pour over with catsup. Let cook 15 – 20 minutes.

* * * * *

BAR-B-QUE

From Lavonne Brandt

2 lb ground goose neck or beef (not too fat)
salt & pepper to taste
1 teaspoon dry mustard
2 tablespoons sugar
2 tablespoons vinegar
1 tablespoon pickling spice (in a bag)
    or in place of pickling spice:
    ¼ teaspoon allspice
    ¼ teaspoon nutmeg
    ¼ teaspoon cloves
    dash of chili powder

1 teaspoon Worchester sauce
1 bottle of catsup (rinse out bottle with
    vinegar and bit of water to get
    everything out of the bottle)
The following to your family's taste:
Onion
Celery
Green pepper

Mix all together and simmer for 1½ - 2 hours

* * * * *

CHICKEN 'N' CASSEROLE

3½ lbs young chicken
Salt, pepper and ginger
¼ cup strained tomatoes
2 tablespoons fat or butter
2 tablespoons flour

Dress, clean, and cut chicken at joints for serving. Season with salt, pepper, and ginger to taste. Dredge with flour and fry in hot fat until brown. Add a little sliced onion and celery and carrot. Place in casserole, covered, and put in slow oven. Simmer 1 hour until tender and browned. Add a little water and let steam for about 15 minutes.

* * * * *

CHICKEN WITH BROWN RICE

From Mrs. Hilda Spain   Minneapolis, MN

Leftover chicken takes on new dimensions when it is combined with brown rice and other tasty ingredients. This would be a good dish to make ahead and serve at a Sunday night buffet party. You're friends won't know how healthy they're getting, but they surely will enjoy it.

4 cups brown rice, cooked
3 tablespoons soy oil
¼ cup rice flour
½ teaspoon paprika
½ teaspoon celery powder

2 cups nut milk
1 cup chicken broth
3 cups chopped cooked chicken
1 cup mushrooms
¼ cup pimiento strips

Add 1 tablespoon oil to cooked rice; set aside. In a 3 quart saucepan place rest of oil, stir in flour, paprika and celery powder. Remove from heat and gradually stir in milk and chicken broth. Cook over medium heat, stirring constantly until thickened. Add chicken, mushrooms, pimiento and rice; heat thoroughly. Place in shallow casserole and garnish with parsley.

* * * * *

CHICKEN-PECAN SPREAD

From Ruth Schwartz

Serve this delicious spread at your next party – with turnip slices, cucumber slices or stuffed in celery sticks and your weight-watching friends will love you.

2 cups cooked chicken, minced
¼ cup finely chopped celery
1 pimiento, finely chopped

½ cup chopped pecans
1 tablespoon fresh lime juice
homemade mayonnaise

Combine all ingredients and add enough mayonnaise to suit individual taste. Place mixture in a glass bowl and sprinkle liberally with parsley flakes.

* * * * *

CHILI CON CARNE

1 lb ground beef
1 cup elbow spaghetti (cooked)
1 can tomatoes
1 can tomato soup

1 medium onion, minced
1 cup diced celery
1 can red kidney beans
Salt, pepper, chili powder to taste.

Fry onions and meat until meat is well seared. Add tomatoes, tomato soup, celery and seasoning and simmer for 30 – 60 minutes or until flavors are well blended. Add spaghetti and kidney beans during last 10 minutes of cooking.

* * * * *

CHILI CON CARNE

Brown 1 lb ground beef in 1 tablespoon fat.
Add
1 cup diced onion
1 clove garlic, chopped fine
½ cup green pepper, diced
Cook until onions are transparent.

Add
2 cups canned tomatoes (or equivalent in fresh tomatoes)
chili powder to suit taste
Mix together and add:
2 tablespoon cold water
1 teaspoon salt
1 teaspoon sugar
1 teaspoon Worchester sauce

Cover and simmer 1 hour.
Add 1 can drained dark red kidney beans and cook 1 hour uncovered.

* * * * *

CHINESE RICE

From Mrs. Hilda Spain Minneapolis, MN

A hearty meal in a dish – easy to prepare

3 cups cooked brown rice, chilled
2 tablespoons corn oil
¾ cup sliced scallions
1 teaspoon sea salt

1½ cups cooked julienne cut chicken
1 egg, beaten
3 tablespoons minced parsley
1 tablespoon soy sauce

Heat oil in skillet, stir in rice until browned. Mix in scallions, sea salt, and chicken for 1 minute.
Make a well in center of rice and pour the egg into it, stirring until barely set, then stir into the
rice mixture. Add parsley and soy sauce and stir, cook only 1 minute.

* * * * *

CHOP SUEY

Use any of the following:
Beef & gravy
Turkey & gravy
Pork & gravy
Chicken & gravy

Put gravy in skillet, thin gravy with bean sprout juice.
Add:
Celery, sliced
Onions
Mushroom, sliced (if desired)

Cook celery until tender.
Add ¼ cup soy sauce
½ tablespoon brown sauce

Add meat leftover (cut up) and 1 can drained bean sprouts.

Blend 3 tablespoons corn starch and ¼ cup cold water.

Cook rice separately and serve the above over the rice.

* * * * *

CHOW MEIN OR SHOP SUEY

2 cups sliced onions
2 cups celery
1 tablespoon vegetable oil
2 cups diced leftover cooked meat or
    poultry

2 cups chicken broth or 2 chicken bouillon
    cubes dissolved in 2 cups boiling
    water
3 tablespoons soy sauce
1 tablespoon molasses
1 can (19 ounces) bean sprouts, drained
3 tablespoons cornstarch

Chow mein noodles or hot cooked rice

Sauté onions and celery in the oil until crisp-tender. Add next 5 ingredients. Simmer 5 – 10 minutes. Stir in cornstarch blended with a small amount of cold water and cook, stirring, until thickened. Serve on noodles for Chow Mein or rice for Chop Suey. Makes 4-6 servings.

* * * * *

CONCORDIA MACARONI

1/3 box macaroni

Cook macaroni in salt water the usual way for 8 people.

Make 2 cups of cheese sauce by melting ½ cup cut up cheese in ordinary thin white sauce stirring till smooth.
Boil and coarsely chop two eggs.
Place macaroni in a well buttered baking dish (one layer) sprinkle over it a layer of chopped eggs, add a liberal amount of sauce till all is used. Cover with crumbs and dot with butter and brown in oven. Sometimes if you have peas, or cooked asparagus, add to the sauce before mixing in baking pan.

* * * * *

EGG FOO YOUNG

Squash is a good source of vitamin A. Its low calorie status makes it especially appealing to weight-watchers. This is a good supper dish – with fresh fruit and a tossed salad.

4 medium unpeeled zucchini squash
    (grated)
1 onion (grated)

3 beaten eggs
1 teaspoon sea salt
½ cup wheat germ

Mix together. Drop by tablespoon on heated griddle or bake on a cookie sheet in oven.

* * * * *

ENTRECOTE MARCHAND DE VIN (Steak with Wine Sauce)

From Eagle Supermarket

4 steaks, sirloin, porterhouse or T-bone
2 teaspoon minced shallots or onions
1/3 cup red wine, preferably Bordeaux
1 pinch salt

1 pinch pepper
¾ stick of butter
1 teaspoon olive oil

Preparation and Cooking:
Heat half of butter and oil in a frying pan. Cook the meat 10 minutes on each side, then salt and pepper it. Remove the meat from the pan. Keep warm in oven. Place the wine and shallots in a small saucepan. Heat over low fire till reduced to 2/3. Off the fire, beat in the remaining butter to thicken the sauce.

Presentation:
Place steaks in middle of a platter. Garnish with small steamed potatoes that have been rolled in butter and parsley. Pour wine sauce over the steaks.

* * * * *

FAVORITE PORK CHOP BAKE OF JEANNE'S

6 pork chops
1 egg, beaten
salt and pepper to taste

2 tablespoons melted butter
1 (16 oz) can cream style corn
6 oz milk

Trim pork chops (browning of pork chops optional). Lay pork chops in 9 x 13 pan. Beat egg; add milk with salt and pepper. Add butter to corn and blend with beaten egg mixture. Pour over pork chops. Bake at 350 degrees for 1½ hour or until tender.

* * * * *

HAMBURG STROGANOFF

From Linda

Melt in a heavy skillet:
¼ cup butter
Add and cook slowly until soft:
½ cup minced onion

Add:
1 pound ground beef
Season with garlic
Stir until lightly browned.

Stir in:
2 tablespoons flour
1 teaspoon salt
¼ teaspoon pepper
½ pound mushrooms sliced (or 1 can of sliced mushrooms)
Cook 5 minutes.

Add:
1 can cream of mushroom soup.
Simmer 10 minutes. Stir in
1 cup sour cream

Heat, taste and add more salt if needed. Sprinkle with parsley, chives or dill.
(May stir in a little curry instead).

Serve this over egg noodles that have a little butter melted on them and have been sprinkled with poppy seeds.

* * * * *

HAM FINGERS

From Mary Lanz

¾ lb smoked ham
1½ lb fresh pork
¾ cup bread crumbs
2 eggs

Shape in fingers and place in baking dish. Pour over sauce and bake one hour.

Sauce:

4 tablespoons brown sugar
2 tablespoons vinegar
1½ teaspoon dry mustard
1 cup water

* * * * *

HAM LOAF

From Violet

2 # Pork (shoulder)
1# raw ham, lean, ground twice
1½ cup milk

2 eggs
1 cup cracker crumbs (no salt)
a little pepper

Butter ring mold or loaf well. Pour 1 can tomato soup over and bake 1½ hour.

* * * * *

HAM LOAF

From Mrs. Rote

(6 loaves)

12# meat (1/3 each of ham, pork and
    veal)
Add 2 loafs bread (12 cups)
3 cans tomato soup

moisten bread with 2 cups milk
9 eggs
6 green peppers ground with meat

Bake 2 hours (no longer).

Mustard Sauce

½ can bouillon or 2 bouillon cubes
½ cup sugar
½ cup vinegar, diluted
½ cup prepared mustard

¼ cup butter
1 teaspoon flour
yolks of 3 eggs, beaten

* * * * *

HEALTH-FULL CHOP SUEY

From V. A. Arsenault Andover, MA

An economical main dish that's delicious and nutritious. In a large pot:

Sauté lightly in 3 tablespoons corn oil for 5 minutes:
3 medium onions, chopped
4 large stalks celery, sliced thin
¾ pound sandwich steaks cut in 1 inch wide strips (may be omitted if vegetable dish only is desired)

Then:
Add 1 pound fresh mung bean sprouts over all ingredients.
Cover with water to 1 ½ inches over all ingredients. (Water will provide gravy so put at level you desire.) Simmer 1 hour, covered.

Mix: 2 tablespoons blackstrap molasses
1/3 cup soy sauce
3 tablespoons corn starch (level) mixed with enough cold water to make a smooth paste.

Add to pot mixture, stir well. Simmer 20 more minutes. If too thin, add additional corn starch and cold water.
Serve over brown rice.   Add soy sauce to taste.
If desired, add last:
½ cup sliced mushrooms
½ cup water chestnuts

* * * * *

HOLIDAY SCRAPPLE

LEFT OVER TURKEY OR CHICKEN

This is a great way to put the remains of the holiday bird to good nutritional use. Makes a wonderful high protein breakfast that the children can easily heat and serve themselves. If your children are accustomed to putting syrup on their scrapple, give them pure maple syrup or raw honey.

2 cups corn meal
1 cup wheat germ
1 cup chicken or turkey broth
1 teaspoon chopped onion
1 cup chopped celery
2 tablespoons chopped green pepper

1 cup canned tomatoes
2 cups ground cooked chicken or turkey
¾ cup ground almonds
mayonnaise
seasoning to taste

Mix corn meal and wheat germ with broth and cook in top of double boiler until mixture is thick. Add onion and cook 10 minutes. Add celery, green pepper, tomatoes, and chicken or turkey. Mix almonds with a little mayonnaise and add to the chicken or turkey mixture. Add sea salt or kelp to suit taste. Put into an oblong dish and place in refrigerator for a few hours or overnight. Slice and brown.

★ ★ ★ ★ ★

INDIAN PILAU

From Mrs. R. W. Hartmann Ft. Meyers, FL

A hearty tasty crunchy side dish for a buffet supper, a backyard picnic or a 'covered dish' party.

3 cups uncooked brown rice
6½ cups chicken broth
3 tablespoons olive oil
1 teaspoon ground allspice

2 sticks cinnamon
6 tablespoons chopped almonds
¾ cup raisins

Put the rice, chicken broth, olive oil, allspice, cinnamon in a flat baking dish. Mix well. Cover and bake in oven (350 degrees) for 50 minutes, or until the liquid has been absorbed and the grains are separated. Stir in the almonds and raisins. Remove cinnamon sticks. Mix well and serve.

★ ★ ★ ★ ★

JELLIED VEAL LOAF

From Mildred Ekberg Mesa, AZ

An attractive dish to make ahead for a buffet dinner

2 breasts of veal
1 bunch carrots
1 cup diced celery
1 teaspoon sea salt

1 medium onion
¼ teaspoon powdered kelp
½ teaspoon summer savory

Cover veal with water; add the celery, onion, sea salt, powdered kelp and summer savory. Cook until the meat comes easily from the bones. Strain stock and cook down to one cup. Oil mold, line with the steamed sliced carrots, then a layer of veal, etc, until all are used. Pour over the cup of stock and press down. Chill until set. Serve unmolded on platter garnished with some of the choice celery leaves.

* * * * *

LIVER CANAPE

From Mrs. Donald Fitz Harrisburg, PA

We're always glad for recipes that use liver and the organ meats. This is a slightly different version of the ever-popular chopped liver. The caraway seed gives it a taste of rye without the bread. Instead of crackers, try it stuffed in celery or spread on turnip or cucumber slices.

4 pieces of cooked baby liver (beef)
½ cup onion
1/8 cup soy oil
1/8 cup olive oil

1/8 portion of garlic clove
¼ teaspoon caraway seeds
½ teaspoon chives
dash savory

Blend above ingredients in blender and spread on crackers. Also delicious as an appetizer on a bed of lettuce, one small ice cream dipper for each serving – luscious!

* * * * *

LIVER PATTIES

Liver gets a 'pick me up' nibble status and goes to a party

1 pound beef or steer liver
1 medium onion
½ medium green pepper
small clove of garlic

Put above through meat grinder or chop
    fine in wooden bowl. Add:
a little sea salt
¼ cup wheat germ
1 egg

Mix well and drop by teaspoonful into pan in which 1 tablespoon of corn oil has been heated. Brown well on both sides.

* * * * *

52

LIVER-VEAL LOAF

½ lb beef liver
1 pint boiling water
1 medium onion, diced
1½ lb boneless veal, ground
2 eggs slightly beaten

1 cup tomato sauce
½ cup wheat germ (or more)
1/8 teaspoon sage
sea salt to taste

In a bowl, pour the boiling water over the liver and let stand for 10 minutes. Drain off the water and cut the liver coarsely. Grind liver with the onion, using a medium blade. Combine with the ground veal. Add tomato sauce, seasoning, eggs, and wheat germ. Mix thoroughly and pack into an oiled loaf pan. Bake in a moderate oven for 1½ hours. Serve hot, accompanied by a mixed green salad.

* * * * *

LIVER WITH AVOCADO

From Prevention Magazine

1 pound calves (or baby beef) liver, thinly
    sliced
1 large ripe avocado, sliced
sea salt

freshly ground black pepper
3 tablespoons cold pressed oil
2 tablespoons lemon juice
1/3 cup water

Sauté slices of liver in oil, slowly over medium heat until brown. Remove from pan and place in covered serving dish. Sauté avocado slices in the same pan until slightly browned, and then arrange them over the liver. Add a little water, sea salt and freshly ground black pepper.

To the leavings in the pan add a little water and bring to boil, stirring until reduced to a glaze. Pour this over the liver and avocado. Then sprinkle with lemon juice and serve accompanied by brown rice and a green salad.

* * * * *

MACARONI

Break ½ cup of macaroni into inch pieces after washing. Put into 3 pints of boiling salted boiling water and keep boiling 50 minutes. Put into a colander and drain. Pour cold water through it to cleanse and cool. Put into a baking dish and cover with the following sauce after stirring into it a cup of grated cheese.

Sauce For Macaroni

1¼ cups of very fresh milk
1 tablespoon butter

1 tablespoon flour
½ teaspoon salt

Cook and spoon over macaroni and sprinkle top with ¾ cup cracker crumbs. Bake till brown.

 * * * * *

MEAT LOAF

From Mrs. V. C. Vann Murfreesboro, NC

Meat loaf is always hearty fare. This one combines the good protein of meat with the wonderful nutrients in wheat germ and brewer's yeast. If your hamburger mixture contains some organ meat like lung and heart, it will be even more nutritious.

1½ pounds ground beef
¾ cup oatmeal uncooked
3 teaspoons brewer's yeast
3 tablespoons wheat germ

1 egg beaten
¼ cup chopped onion
1½ teaspoons sea salt or kelp
1½ cups tomato juice

Combine all ingredients; pack firmly in an ungreased 8 ½ x 4 ½ x 2 ½ pan. Bake in a preheated oven at 350 degrees for 1 hour and 15 minutes. Let stand 5 minutes before slicing. Makes 8 servings.

* * * * *

MEAT LOAF

From Ella E. Copelan Sweet Home, OR

Be prepared for seconds. This nutrition-packed main dish has a zesty goodness your family will enjoy.

1 pound hamburger
2 large eggs
½ teaspoon sea salt
1 teaspoon bone meal
2 tablespoons brewer's yeast
1 cup sunflower meal

½ cup onion
¼ teaspoon pepper
1 teaspoon dolomite
½ teaspoon fresh sage
1 teaspoon kelp

Put all but hamburger in blender. Blend well. Then add to meat and mix well. Form in loaf and bake at 300 degrees until done, about 1 hour.

Variations:

1. Add tomato puree instead of soy milk. *[EDITOR'S NOTE: This recipe had several typos despite the fact it came from a publication – I checked the ingredients several times. There was no soy milk listed. Good luck!]*
2. Add chopped olives and pimentos
3. Add chopped pickle
4. Add ½ cup ground carrots
5. Put a row of peeled, hard-boiled eggs through the middle.
6. Put a one-inch layer of sliced parsnips in bottom. Put in half of meat, then another layer of parsnips and then last half of meat.
7. Layer sliced green peppers the same as the parsnips.

* * * * *

MEXICAN CASSEROLE

½ lb hamburger
1 medium onion
¼ teaspoon salt
½ lb chili

½ can tomato soup
1 med. pkg Fritos
½ cup grated cheese
Dash of catsup

Brown hamburger, and then simmer till done. Add chopped onion and salt. Mix chili and soup into meat. Let simmer while stirring. Mixture should be consistency of gravy. If dry, add small amount of water. Line large casserole with ½ of Fritos. Pour in meat mixture, then rest of Fritos on top. Sprinkle cheese and catsup on top. Bake until cheese is melted at 400 degrees.

* * * * *

MUSTARD SAUCE FOR HAM LOAF

½ can bouillon
½ cup sugar
½ cup vinegar diluted
½ cup prepared mustard

¼ cup butter
1 teaspoon flour
3 egg yolks beaten

Bring to a boil in a double boiler.

* * * * *

ONION SAVORY CASSEROLE

Cook small whole onions till tender in salted water. Make cream sauce adding 2 hard boiled eggs chopped, chopped diced (small) meat, and half cup cheese cut up. Pour over onions. Dot butter over the top before baking. Bake till crumbs on top are brown.

* * * * *

RICE AND VEGETABLE CASSEROLE

3 cups brown rice, uncooked
2 carrots, diced small
1 bell pepper, diced small

2 tomatoes diced
6 eggs, hard boiled
1 tomato, blended with juice from ½ lemon

Cook brown rice, when rice is almost cooked and some water still remains,
Add vegetables, (carrots, peppers, diced tomato)
Chop hard-boiled eggs finely, add tomato juice with lemon and heat. Pour over rice and vegetables in serving plate. Sprinkle with raw wheat germ.
Serves 6

* * * * *

SALMON LOAF WITH CREAMY DILL SAUCE

From Good HouseKeeping

2 tablespoons salad oil
¾ cup finely chopped celery
½ cup fresh or frozen chopped onion
1 (7 ¾ oz) can salmon
1 egg

1 (5.33 oz) can evaporated milk
1 cup fresh bread crumbs
1 teaspoon salt
¼ teaspoon pepper

About 1½ hour before serving or the day ahead –
In a 2 quart sauce pan over medium high heat, in hot salad oil, cook celery and onion until tender (about 10 minutes). Remove saucepan from heat and add salmon and its liquid and remaining ingredients except Dill Sauce. With fork or pastry blender combine mixture until well mixed and smooth. Grease 6 x 3 ½ loaf pan or 2 cup ovenproof bowl. Spoon salmon mixture evenly into the pan. Bake in 350 degree oven for 50 minutes or until knife inserted in center comes out clean. Remove loaf from pan. Serve hot or cold with Dill Sauce.

Dill Sauce

In small bowl, with wire whisk combine and mix until smooth:
½ cup mayonnaise
¼ cup sour cream
1 tablespoon lemon juice
1 tablespoon milk

2 teaspoons finely chopped fresh dill (or 1
    teaspoon dill weed)
½ teaspoon salt
½ teaspoon sugar
1/8 teaspoon pepper

Refrigerate Dill Sauce until ready to serve.

* * * * *

SAVORY MACARONI

Prepare macaroni as usual by boiling 40-50 minutes in salted water. Make a Creole sauce as follows:

Mix 6 fresh ripe tomatoes (or 1 cup canned tomatoes)
1 onion cut fine and fried 2-3 minutes in a tablespoon finely cut up bacon.
2 cloves and salt to taste.

Cook till thick, stirring often. Add 1 teaspoon sugar and ½ cup minced meat. Pour over macaroni. Mix delicately. Grate cheese over top and bake until a rich brown.

* * * * *

SCALLOPED POTATOES AND HAM

3 tablespoons butter
4½ cups spuds
1 cup onion
3 tablespoons flour

½ teaspoon pepper
2 cups milk
2 or 3 cups ham

Melt butter then add flour and pepper. Add milk slowly and allow to thicken. Slice spuds, dice onion. Layer spuds, onion and ham in baking dish. Pour white sauce over all. Bake 425 degrees for 45 – 60 minutes or until done.

* * * * *

SLOW COOKER CHILI

Be sure to drain the beans thoroughly.

2 pounds beef chuck, cut in ½ to 1 inch
    cubes
Large onion, chopped medium-fine
1 (8 oz) can tomato sauce

2 cans (each 1 pound) red kidney beans,
    well-drained
1½ - 2 tablespoons chili powder
Tabasco pepper sauce to taste (½ – ¾
    teaspoon)

In an electric slow cooker stir together all the ingredients. Cover and cook on high for 4 – 5 hours or on low for 8 – 10 hours or until beef is tender. Makes 6 servings.

* * * * *

STEAK SUPREME

From Linda

2½ lb sirloin (½ in thick)
½ cup flour
2 eggs
1 cup soda cracker crumbs
½ cup grated parmesan cheese
½ teaspoon pepper

¼ cup parsley flakes
1 teaspoon garlic salt
1 teaspoon onion salt
1 cup oil
½ cup water

1. Cut steak into 3 in squares, dust with flour.
2. Beat eggs slightly w/milk in pie plate. Combine cracker crumbs, cheese, pepper, parsley, garlic and onion salts in second pie plate. Dip meat into egg mixture, then into crumb mixture to coat evenly.
3. In frying pan, heat oil on medium-low heat. Brown meat slowly. Remove from heat.
4. Meat into casserole dish. Add water. Bake covered in a preheated 300 degree oven for 1 hour 15 minutes, (or until tender.)

 * * * * *

VEGETABLES

BARBECUED LIMA BEANS

6 cups water
2 cups large-size dried lima beans
½ pound bacon, cut up
1 medium-sized onion, chopped
Garlic salt, to taste
2 tablespoons butter
1½ teaspoons chili powder

1 can condensed tomato soup
2 teaspoons Worchester sauce
2 teaspoons prepared mustard
¼ cup brown sugar, packed
¼ cup cider vinegar
Salt to taste
Bacon slices

Place water, beans, one-half pound cut-up bacon, onion, and garlic salt in a large kettle or pan. Bring to a boil, then reduce heat and simmer for one and a half hours.

When beans are firm but fork-tender (do not overcook or they will become mushy), drain reserving juice.

* * * * *

★ CORN SOUFFLE

From Jean (Doris Thompson)

Blend together in
saucepan over medium
heat:
¼ cup butter, melted
½ teaspoon onion
¼ cup flour

Remove from heat. Mix
in:
1 can corn, cream style
(1 lb, 1 oz)
½ teaspoon salt

Beat together:
3 egg yolks
2/3 cup milk
dash of Tabasco

Mix the egg yolk mixture with the corn.

Beat 3 egg whites and fold into above mixture.
Pour in buttered casserole dish. Top with 1/8 green pepper.
Bake 350 degrees for 45 minutes.

* * * * *

SCALLOPED CORN

1 whole corn
1 cream style corn
2 eggs
¼ cup milk

Bread crumbs to mixture
Bake in oven
Strips of green pepper on top

* * * * *

PRETTY SPROUTS

From Mrs. Harry Lundquist Marysville, WN

Spouts in the raw are so chuck full of valuable nutrients, we're delighted to suggest a new way to use them.

1 pound bean sprouts
liquid from pint of homemade pickled beets
2 tablespoons minced onion
2 tablespoons wheat germ

¼ cup sunflower seeds coarsely chopped
   or use sunflower meal
1 hard cooked egg, sieved or mashed with
   fork
homemade mayonnaise

Marinate sprouts all day in beet liquid. Drain well. Add remaining ingredients except egg, which is to be used as garnish. The beet liquid makes the spouts a pretty color and also gives them a good flavor.

* * * * *

SOUTHERN GREEN BEANS

3 slices bacon
½ cup finely chopped green onions
1 cup cubed cooked ham
1½ pounds fresh green beans, broken into
2 inch lengths

Boiling, salted water
2 tablespoons chopped fresh parsley
Dash hot pepper sauce

Fry bacon until crisp; drain on paper towels. Add onions and ham to bacon drippings and cook until onions are tender. Remove from heat and reserve.

Cook beans in small amount of boiling salted water, covered, until just tender, about 15 minutes. Drain.

Crumble bacon. Combine bacon, ham-onion mixture, parsley and hot pepper sauce. Toss with beans.

Yield: Four to six servings.

* * * * *

SPINACH SWINGER

2 envelops Knox Unflavored gelatin
1 (10-oz) can condensed beef broth
¼ cup water
½ teaspoon salt
2 tablespoons lemon juice
1 cup salad dressing

1 (10-oz) frozen chopped spinach, thawed
¼ cup chopped green onion
4 hard-cooked eggs, chopped
½ pound crispy bacon, crumbled
pimiento strips

Soften gelatin in beef broth. Stir over low heat until dissolved. Stir in water, salt and lemon juice. Gradually add gelatin to salad dressing, mixing until well blended. Chill until slightly thickened. Fold in spinach, onion, eggs and bacon. Pour into 1 ½ quart mold. Chill until firm. Unmold and garnish with pimiento strips. 8 servings.

* * * * *

SWEET POTATO BOATS

From Dan Morris San Jose, Calif

They look great, taste wonderful, and delight the children who love the boat shape. They are especially good with turkey.

3 large sweet potatoes
1 cup fresh cranberries
¼ cup raisins

½ cup walnuts
½ cup sesame seeds

Cook whole sweet potatoes in their jackets just until tender. Cut in half lengthwise, spoon out center of sweet potato halves and mash. Put remaining ingredients through the chopper. Mix with the mashed sweet potato. Fill the sweet potato with the mixture. Bake at 350 degrees for 30 minutes.

* * * * *

★ TOMATO-VEGETABLE COCKTAIL

From Jean (Family Circle Magazine)

Wash and core 12 large ripe tomatoes, chop
Combine with
½ cup chopped carrots
½ cup chopped celery
½ cup chopped onion

Add
2 teaspoons salt
2 tablespoons lemon juice
1 teaspoon Worchester sauce
dash of Tabasco sauce

Bring to boiling, lower heat slightly and cook rapidly for 25 minutes or until vegetables are tender. Press through strainer or food mill. Ladle into quart jars, leaving ¼ inch headroom. Seal. Process 15 minutes in water bath. Makes 2 quarts.

NOTE: Add 1 teaspoon lemon juice for every quart jar of tomatoes.

* * * * *

THREE BEAN CASSEROLE

From Mrs. Wendell Millard, Platteville

8 slices bacon
1 cup finely diced celery
1½ cup chopped onion
1 cup water
1 (6 ounce) can tomato paste
½ cup brown sugar, packed
1 package spaghetti sauce mix
2 tablespoons prepared mustard

1 teaspoon garlic salt
2 tablespoons vinegar
2 (8¾ ounce) cans large lima beans
1 (8¾ ounce) can kidney beans, well drained
1 (21 ounce) can pork and beans in tomato sauce

Cook bacon until crisp; drain on absorbent paper. Pour off all but 2 tablespoons of fat. Add celery and onion to fat; sauté five minutes. Add water and next six ingredients. Blend and bring to a boil.

Combine beans in a three quart casserole. Add bacon. Stir in tomato mixture and blend well.

Bake uncovered in a moderate oven (350 degrees) 1 – 1 ½ hours.

Yield: 6 servings.

* * * * *

CAKES

APPLESAUCE CAKE (EGGLESS)

1 cup sugar
½ cup margarine
½ teaspoon cloves
½ teaspoon nutmeg
½ cup chopped nuts

1 teaspoon cinnamon
1 teaspoon soda
1 cup unsweetened applesauce
2 cups flour
½ cup raisins

Mix all of the above together. Put in a greased square pan and bake at 350 degrees until done.

* * * * *

APPLE SAUCE CAKE

1 cup sugar
1 cup raisins
½ cup shortening
2 cups flour
1½ cups unsweetened apple sauce

1 teaspoon soda
1 teaspoon cloves
2 teaspoons lukewarm water
1 teaspoon cinnamon

Cream butter and sugar. Add applesauce. Dissolve soda in water. Sift flour twice and add. Bake in oven slowly.

* * * * *

★ BANANA NUT CAKE

1½ cup sugar
1½ cup nuts
1 teaspoon soda
3 mashed bananas
2 teaspoon baking powder
1 teaspoon vanilla

2 eggs
½ cup milk
2 cup flour
½ cup shortening
salt

Bake in a 350 degree oven for 35 minutes.

* * * * *

★ BOILED RAISIN CAKE

From Geigel Prien

Good

Boil 15 minutes:
1 cup raisins
2 cups water

Let cool. Measure liquid from raisins and if you don't have 1 cupful add water to equal 1 cup.

When cool put the raisins and the 1 cup liquid in a bowl and add:

1 cup sugar	1 teaspoon cinnamon
¼ cup shortening	1 teaspoon cloves
1 egg	1 teaspoon salt
1¾ cup flour	1 teaspoon soda

Beat well. Bake in a loaf pan.
NOTES: "I use a 350 degree oven. I sprinkle a little sugar on top before putting in oven. Makes it have sort of a crisp top, as I do not frost it. Nutmeats add to batter make a better cake but recipe doesn't call for any. Vanilla may also be added if desired."

* * * * *

BUTTERMILK RHUBARB CAKE

From Mrs. Arthur Hartwig

1½ cups brown sugar	1 teaspoon soda
1 cup butter	1 teaspoon vanilla
1 cup buttermilk	2 cups flour
1 egg	1½ cup finely cut rhubarb

Mix as for cake: beat until smooth, adding rhubarb last. Put in 9 x 13 pan, greased and floured. (Batter will be thick.)

Cover with topping:
½ cup sugar
1 teaspoon cinnamon

Bake at 350 degrees about 30 minutes. Serve with whipped cream or ice cream.

* * * * *

BUTTERMILK SPICE CAKE (EGGLESS)

1 cup buttermilk
1 cup sugar
1 cup chopped raisins
¼ cup margarine
2 cups flour

1 rounded teaspoon soda
1 teaspoon nutmeg
1 teaspoon cloves
1 teaspoon cinnamon

Beat all together and bake in an 8 inch square pan. Bake slowly in 350 degree oven.
(If oven runs hot, then use 325 degrees.)

* * * * *

CAKE FOR SOUR CREAM NUT FILLING

Whites of 5 eggs
2 cups sugar
1 scant cup butter

1 cup sweet milk
3 teaspoons baking powder
3 cups sifted flour

Bake in layers

For Filling:

Yolks of 5 eggs
1 cup sour cream
1 cup powdered sugar

1 cup chopped nuts
Almond flavoring

Cook creamed sugar and eggs then add nuts and flavoring. Do not let eggs cook long enough
to curdle but make like boiled custard.

* * * * *

CARROT PECAN CAKE

1¼ cup oil
2 cups sugar
2 cups flour
1 teaspoon baking soda
2 teaspoons baking powder

2 teaspoons cinnamon
1 teaspoon salt
4 eggs
3 cups grated raw carrots
1 cup finely chopped pecans

Combine oil and sugar, mixing well. Sift together flour, soda, baking powder, cinnamon and salt. Sift half of dry ingredients into sugar mixture and blend. Sift in remaining dry ingredients alternately with eggs, one at a time. Mix well after each addition. Add carrots and mix well, then stir in pecans. Pour into lightly oiled 10 inch tube pan. Bake at 325 degrees for 1 hour and 10 minutes. Cool in pan upright and top with orange glaze. Makes one cake.

Orange glaze:

1 cup sugar
¼ cup cornstarch
1 teaspoon fresh lemon juice
1 cup fresh orange juice

½ teaspoon salt
2 tablespoons grated orange peel
2 tablespoons butter

Combine sugar, cornstarch in saucepan. Add lemon and orange juice slowly and stir until smooth. Add remaining ingredients. Cook over low heat until thick and glossy. Split cake into three horizontal layers. Spread orange glaze between and on top and sides.

* * * * *

CINNAMON STREUSEL CAKE

1 package Duncan Hines Deluxe II Yellow Cake Mix
1 package vanilla instant pudding mix (4 serving size)

2 tablespoons oil
1 1/3 cups water
2 eggs

Streusel:

½ cup flour
½ cup brown sugar

2 teaspoons cinnamon
2 tablespoons butter or margarine, melted

Preheat oven to 375 degrees. In large bowl blend cake mix, pudding mix, oil, water and eggs. Beat 2 minutes at medium speed. Spread ¾ of batter evenly in greased and floured 10 inch tube pan. Combine streusel ingredients. Sprinkle 2/3 cup of mixture over batter in pan. Spread remaining batter over streusel; top with reserved streusel. Bake 40 – 50 minutes at 375 degrees until done. Cool right side up 25 minutes. Remove from pan and glaze top side up.

Glaze:

Blend ¾ cup confectioners sugar with about 1 tablespoon milk; drizzle over cake.

* * * * *

DARK CAKE (EGGLESS)

1 cup raisins boiled in 3 cups water – Let cool.
  (Save liquid from raisins to equal 1 cup)

Cream together:
2 heaping tablespoons margarine
2 cups sugar

Add raisins and 1 cup liquid

Sift together:
2 cups flour	1 teaspoon cloves
1 teaspoon soda	1 teaspoon nutmeg
1 teaspoon baking powder	1 teaspoon salt
1 teaspoon cinnamon	

Mix everything together and bake in a 9 x 13 pan in 350 degree oven.

* * * * *

DARK FRUIT CAKE

From Mrs. George R. Barry, Monroe

½ pound butter	½ pound candied cherries
½ cup brown sugar	½ pound candied pineapple
½ cup white sugar	¼ pound citron peel
6 eggs	1/8 pound lemon peel
¼ cup light molasses	½ cup maraschino cherries
1/8 cup fruit juice	1 cup sifted flour
1/8 cup lemon juice	¼ teaspoon soda
1 pound seeded raisins	1½ teaspoons cinnamon
1 package dates	¼ teaspoon cloves
¾ pound blanched almonds	¼ teaspoon allspice
½ pound currants	¼ teaspoon nutmeg

Shave fruit peel. Sliver almonds; cut cherries in half, dates in fifths; leave pineapple in large pieces. Brandy may be added to fruit (½ cup) if desired. Cream butter and sugar; add eggs, the molasses and juices. Add fruits and nuts to sifted dry ingredients, and then mix with wet mixture. Pour into pans lined with 2 sheets brown paper, and greased. Bake in 250 degree oven, covered with foil for 1½ hour, and then uncovered for 1½ hour. When cool, brush with brandy and wrap tightly in foil or in plastic bag.

 * Note: Advised to make the fruit cake early – it is better when it ages.

* * * * *

66

DARK FRUIT CAKE

From Ila Gordan – Mrs. Rote

2 cups butter (1/2 butter, ½ Crisco)
2 cups brown sugar
3 cups flour
2 cups chopped raisins
2 cups currants
½ cup Angela
1 cup chopped walnut meats
1 cup blanched almonds
1 cup candied cherries

1 cup candied pineapple
½ cup figs
11 eggs beaten
½ cup wine or brandy
2 teaspoons cinnamon
1 teaspoon cloves
1 teaspoon cream of tartar
½ teaspoon soda
1 teaspoon lemon extract

Add flour last. Bake 4 hours or less.

* * * * *

DATE AND WALNUT CAKE

2 tablespoons butter
1 cup sugar
1 egg
¾ lb dates

1 cup hot water
1 teaspoon soda
1½ cups flour (scant)
½ lb walnut meats

* * * * *

FAST FIXIN FRUIT 'N' CAKE

1 package Duncan Hines Deluxe II White Cake Mix
¼ cup oil
2 eggs
½ cup water
1 can (20 – 23 oz) of your favorite pie filling

Preheat oven to 350 degrees. Pour oil into a 13 x 9 x 2 inch pan; tilt pan to cover bottom. Put cake mix, eggs and water into pan. Stir with a fork or spoon until blended (about 2 minutes). Scrape sides and spread batter evenly in pan. Spoon pie filling onto batter. Use a fork to fold into batter just enough to create a marbled effect. Bake at 350 degrees for 35 – 45 minutes, until toothpick inserted near center comes out clean. Cooled cake may be sprinkled with powdered sugar. Use a knife to loosen cake from sides. Cut and serve directly from pan. Store cake loosely covered.

* * * * *

★ FRUIT COCKTAIL CAKE

1 ½ cup flour
1 teaspoon soda
1 tablespoon baking powder
½ teaspoon salt
1 cup sugar

1 egg
1 medium can fruit cocktail (30 oz size)
1 cup brown sugar
½ cup pecans

Sift together flour, soda, baking powder and salt. Add sugar, egg and fruit cocktail. Mix together and pour into 9 x 13 greased pan. Sprinkle top with brown sugar and nuts. Bake in 350 degree oven for about 40 – 45 minutes. Serve with whipped cream.

* * * * *

GERMAN FRUIT CAKE

From Mrs. Roger Markham, Juda

¾ cup butter
2 cups brown sugar
4 eggs, separated
3 cups flour
½ teaspoon cinnamon
½ teaspoon nutmeg
½ teaspoon cloves

½ cup buttermilk
1 teaspoon baking soda
2/3 cup cherry preserves
2/3 cup apricot preserves
2/3 cup pineapple preserves
1 cup chopped nuts
1 teaspoon vanilla

Cream shortening and sugar together, add egg yolks. Put baking soda in the half cup of buttermilk. Then sift other dry ingredients together. Add dry ingredients to creamed mixture with buttermilk. Add vanilla, nuts and preserves. Add whipped egg whites last. Bake in a greased and lightly floured tube pan at 350 degrees for 1 ½ hours.

* * * * *

GINGER CAKE RECIPE

Good

½ cup butter
½ cup light brown sugar
1 cup ginger cake brand molasses
1 teaspoon baking soda dissolved in 1 cup boiling water
1 teaspoon cinnamon

1 teaspoon ginger
½ teaspoon cloves
¼ teaspoon allspice
½ teaspoon salt
2 cups sifted flour
2 eggs well beaten

Stir all well together.
Bake in a moderate oven for 30 minutes.

* * * * *

GOLD TO WHITE LAYER CAKE

1 cup sugar
½ cup butter
3 eggs

½ cup milk
1½ cup flour
3 level teaspoon baking powder

Put all together except eggs. Divide the cake dough. Beat yolks and whites of eggs separately. Put yolks in ½ of the cake dough and the whites in the other half. Flavor the yellow with vanilla and the white with lemon. Bake in separate layer tins. Put together with boiled frosting. Cover the upper layer with 2 squares of melted Baker's Chocolate.

* * * * *

GOLDEN POUND CAKE

1 package Duncan Hines Deluxe II Yellow Cake Mix
1 package vanilla instant pudding mix (4 serving size)

½ cup oil
1 cup water
4 eggs

Preheat oven to 350 degrees. Blend all ingredients in a large bowl. Beat at medium speed for 2 minutes. Bake in a greased and floured 10 inch tube pan at 350 degrees for 45 – 55 minutes, until center springs back when touched lightly. Cool right side up for about 25 minutes, then remove from pan.

Glaze:

Blend 1 cup confectioners sugar with either 2 tablespoons milk or 2 tablespoons lemon juice. Drizzle over cake.

* * * * *

GRAHM CRACKER TORTE

From Mrs. Rote

4 eggs beaten separately
1 cup sugar, added to yolks a little at a time

Grind 1 cup graham crackers
Add 1 teaspoon baking powder to graham crackers
1 cup walnuts ground (Mix all three)
Add to yolks.
Fold in beaten whites

Custard

1 egg
1 tablespoon sugar
1 tablespoon cornstarch
1 cup cream (sweet or sour)
Cook in double boiler and put on torte.

* * * * *

GRANDMA'S RAISIN CAKE

From Tina Kaderly (Daughter of Mr. & Mrs. Sam Kaderly, Juda)

350 degree oven
9 x 13 pan

1½ cups raisins
1 cup water
¾ cup (1½ stick) butter, softened
2 eggs, beaten
½ cup milk
¾ cup sugar

1½ cup sifted flour
1 teaspoon soda
2 teaspoons cinnamon
½ teaspoon cloves
1/8 teaspoon nutmeg
1 cup chopped nuts

Cover raisins with water; simmer 20 minutes or until no water is left. Cool. When cool combine with remaining ingredients except nuts. Mix well. Add nuts and mix. Pour into pan. Bake 30 – 35 minutes. When cooled, lightly sift confectioners sugar over surface of cake.

★ ★ ★ ★ ★

HICKORY NUT CAKE

½ cup butter
1 cup sugar
Whites of 3 eggs
½ cup milk

1½ cup flour
¾ cup chopped hickory meats
1 teaspoon cream of tarter
½ teaspoon soda

Cream butter well with sugar, add whites beaten stiff and beat until smooth. Add milk and flour alternately; add nuts, stir then sprinkle over the cream of tartar and stir in the soda dissolved in 1 teaspoon milk. Beat again and place in well buttered loaf pan.

★ ★ ★ ★ ★

HOT MILK SPONGE CAKE

Use round or square 9 inch pan. Preheat oven 350 degrees.

½ cup milk
2 tablespoons butter
2 eggs
1 cup sugar

1 teaspoon vanilla
1 ¼ cup sifted cake flour
1 ½ teaspoon baking powder
½ teaspoon salt

Generously butter bottom of pan and dust with flour. In a one-quart saucepan, heat milk; add butter. Cool.   In a mixing bowl beat eggs until very thick and lemon-colored. Gradually add sugar and continue beating until smooth. Add vanilla. Sift together flour, baking powder and salt; gradually add egg mixture and mix only until blended. Add milk, stirring quickly only until batter is smooth (will be thin). Pour into pan. Bake 30 – 35 minutes. While warm, top with Broiled Coconut Frosting.

Broiled Coconut Frosting

½ cup (1 stick) butter
¾ cup firmly packed light brown sugar
¼ cup light cream or Half and Half
¾ cup flaked coconut or ½ cup coconut and ¼ cup chopped nuts

In a 1 quart sauce pan, melt butter; mix in brown sugar, cream and coconut. Spread on warm cake. Broil until coconut is brown. Cool cake slightly on wire rack before cutting.

* * * * *

★ HURRY UP CAKE

¾ cup sugar
1 ½ cup sifted flour
¼ teaspoon salt
2 teaspoons baking powder

¼ cup melted shortening
1 egg beaten
¾ cup milk
1 teaspoon flavoring

Sift dry ingredients. Drop egg into shortening, add milk and flavoring. Combine. Stir well; pour into greased layer cake tins. Bake in moderate oven or bake in shallow tin, frost, mark into squares and place half a walnut on each square.

* * * * *

JACK-O-LANTERN CAKE

1 package (1 pound 2 ½ ounces) yellow cake mix
¾ cups canned pumpkin
1 teaspoon cinnamon
Molasses Frosting

Prepare cake batter according to package directions substituting pumpkin for ½ cup of the water. Fold in cinnamon. Pour batter evenly into two greased and floured 1½ quart oven proof bowls. Bake in a moderate oven (350 degrees) about 55 minutes, or until cakes test done. Cool 5 minutes. Remove from bowls and cool thoroughly. Place one cake, rounded side down, on serving plate. Frost top with Molasses Frosting. Place second cake, flat side down, over bottom cake so that cake forms pumpkin shape. Frost outside of cake with remaining frosting. Run spatula down sides of cake for pumpkin effect. Make pumpkin stem and jack-o-lantern features with assorted gumdrops.

Molasses Frosting

2 egg whites
1/3 cup molasses
2/3 cup sugar
1/8 teaspoon salt
2 teaspoons grated orange rind

Combine egg whites, molasses, sugar, salt and orange rind in the top of double boiler. Place over rapidly boiling water and cook, beating constantly with electric mixer, until frosting stands in peaks. Remove from heat. Continue beating until frosting is of spreading consistency.

* * * * *

JELLY ROLL

1 cup sugar
4 egg yolks
3 tablespoons cold water
1 cup flour

1 teaspoon baking powder
1 teaspoon lemon juice or vanilla
4 egg whites beaten stiff and folded in last

Beat egg yolks good then add sugar and beat again. Add cold water and lemon juice or vanilla. Sift flour and baking powder together and add to the mixture. Fold in your stiff egg whites. Bake in a hot oven for 12 minutes. Turn out on a powdered sugar towel and spread with jelly and roll. Work quickly!!

Make sure your jelly roll pan is greased and floured well.

NOTE: Tart jelly is the best!

* * * * *

MANDARIN ORANGE CAKE

From Homemaker Magazine

2 cups flour
2 cups sugar
2 eggs beaten
2 teaspoons soda

1 teaspoon vanilla
2 cups mandarin oranges (drained)
½ cup nuts – optional

Beat well (notice there is no shortening).

Pour into 9 x 13 cake pan, greased only. Bake at 350 degrees for 45 minutes. Glaze.

Glaze:

1 cup brown sugar
4 tablespoons margarine
4 teaspoons milk

Bring to a boil and pour over cake as it comes from oven. Prick cake with fork as you pour.
Serve topped with whipped cream.

* * * * *

OLD FASHIONED CARROT CAKE

1 package carrot cake mix
1 can (8 oz) crushed pineapple
1 can (8.5 oz) sliced carrots, drained
¼ cup water

¼ cup vegetable oil
3 eggs
¼ teaspoon ground nutmeg
Cream Cheese-Raisin Frosting

Heat oven to 350 degrees. Mix all ingredients except frosting in ungreased rectangular pan (9
x 13), with fork, scraping corners frequently, until moistened. Stir vigorously 1 minute; scrape
sides with rubber spatula. Spread in pan. Bake until cake springs back when touched lightly in
center 35 – 40 minutes. Cool. Frost with Cream Cheese-Raisin Frosting.

Cream Cheese-Raisin Frosting

Prepare 1 package Betty Crocker cream cheese and nuts frosting mix as directed. Stir in ½
cup raisins.

* * * * *

ORANGE CAKE

5 eggs, yolks
1½ cups sugar
Juice of 1 orange
Grated rind of orange

2 cups flour
2 teaspoons baking powder
Whites of 3 eggs
½ cup hot water

Beat yolks light, add sugar, and beat again. Then add water, orange juice and part of rind and
flour, sifted 3 times with baking powder. Lastly fold in beaten whites of 3 eggs. Bake in 3
layers in a moderate oven.

* * * * *

PIE PLANT CAKE

1½ cup brown sugar
½ cup butter
 1 egg
1 cup buttermilk
2 cups sifted flour

1 teaspoon soda
1 teaspoon vanilla
½ teaspoon salt
1½ cup chopped pie plant.

Mix as listed and place in 10 x 13 pan.

Top with
1/3 cup sugar
1 tablespoon cinnamon

Bake 50 minutes in 350 degree oven.

* * * * *

★ PLAIN CAKE

¼ cup butter
1 cup sugar
2 eggs, separated
1½ cup flour

2 teaspoons baking powder
1 teaspoon spice or flavoring
½ cup milk

Mix and sift flour, baking powder and spices 3 times. Cream butter and sugar; add beaten yolks then flour mixture and milk. Add the flavoring and beaten egg whites last.

* * * * *

PINEAPPLE UPSIDE DOWN CAKE

Light brown sugar
Pineapple rings
About ½ cup butter, softened
2 cups flour
½ teaspoon salt

2 teaspoons baking powder
1 egg
½ cup milk
Whipped cream

Grease a 9 x 13 inch cake pan and place a one-half inch layer of brown sugar over the bottom of the pan. Place a layer of pineapple rings on top of the brown sugar. Put about one teaspoon of butter in the center of each pineapple ring.

Make a batter by blending the remaining butter with flour, salt, baking powder, egg and milk. Pour batter over pineapples in pan and bake in slow (325 degree) oven for 45 minutes until golden brown.

Turn upside down immediately onto serving plate and serve warm with whipped cream.

Yield: 6 – 8 servings.

* * * * *

PISTACHIO MARBLE CAKE

1 package (2 layer size) yellow cake mix
1 package (4 serving size) Pistachio Instant Pudding and Pie filling
4 eggs
1 cup water
½ cup oil
½ teaspoon almond extract
¼ cup chocolate syrup

Combine cake mix, pudding mix, eggs, water, oil and extract in large mixer bowl. Blend; then beat at medium speed of electric mixer for 2 minutes. Measure 1½ cups batter; stir in chocolate syrup. Spoon batters alternately into a greased and floured 10-inch Bundt or tube pan. Zigzag spatula through batter to marble. Bake at 350 degrees for 50 minutes. Cool 15 minutes; remove from pan and finish cooling or rack. Sprinkle with confectioner's sugar, if desired.

* * * * *

QUICK MIX ONE EGG CAKE

From Nancy

8x8 pan, 375 degree oven

1¼ cup flour
¾ cup sugar
½ teaspoon salt
2 teaspoons baking powder

1/3 cup shortening
½ cup milk
1 teaspoon vanilla
1 egg unbeaten

Grease only the bottom of the pan. Sift flour then measure it. Sift again with the sugar, salt and baking powder. Put in fat and stir until soft in bowl. Add flour mixture, but **don't** mix. Add milk and vanilla and stir carefully. Beat 150 strokes. Add egg and beat 150 more strokes. Put into pan.

* * * * *

RAVE REVIEWS CAKE

1 package (2 layer size) white or yellow cake mix
1 package (4 serving size) Jell-O Vanilla flavored Instant Pudding and Pie Filling
1 1/3 cups water
4 eggs
¼ cup oil
1 1/3 cups (1 packet) Bakers Angel Flake Coconut
1 cup chopped pecans or walnuts

Combing cake mix, pudding mix, water, eggs and oil in large mixer bowl. Blend; beat at medium speed for 4 minutes. Stir in coconut and nuts. Pour into 3 greased, floured 9 inch layer pans. Bake at 350 degrees for 35 minutes. Cool in pans 15 minutes. Remove from pans; finish cooling on racks. Frost tops of layers with Coconut Cream Cheese Frosting and stack.

Coconut Cream Cheese Frosting

Sauté 2 2/3 cups (2 packets) Bakers angel Flake Coconut in 2 tablespoons butter or margarine in skillet until golden brown, stirring constantly. Remove from heat. Spread on absorbent paper and cool. Cream 2 tablespoons butter or margarine with 1 package (8 oz) cream cheese. Add 3½ cups sifted confectioners sugar and 2 teaspoons milk alternately, in small amounts, beating well after each addition. Blend in ½ teaspoon vanilla; stir in 2 cups of the sautéed coconut. Use remaining coconut for garnish. Makes 3 cups.

* * * * *

RHUBARB CAKE

½ cup shortening
1½ cups sugar
½ teaspoon salt
1 egg
1 teaspoon baking soda in 1 cup of sour milk (to sour milk, add 2 tablespoons vinegar to milk
    and let stand a few minutes)
2 cups plus 1 tablespoon flour
3 cups rhubarb, cut very fine
¼ cup colored candy sprinkles

Cream together, shortening and 1½ cups sugar in mixing bowl. Add salt and egg; blend. Add sour milk alternately with flour. Stir in rhubarb and candy sprinkles.

Pour batter into a 9 x 13 lightly greased pan. Sprinkle on topping. Bake in a moderate (350 degree) oven 45 minutes.

Topping:

½ cup sugar (white or brown)
½ cup chopped nuts
1 teaspoon cinnamon

Mix in bowl and sprinkle on cake.

* * * * *

RHUBARB CRUNCH CAKE

1½ cups brown sugar
½ cup butter
1 egg
1 cup buttermilk or sour milk

2 cups all purpose flour, sifted
1 teaspoon soda
½ teaspoon salt
1½ cup rhubarb, cut fine

Cream butter and sugar together. Add remaining ingredients in order given. Put into buttered 9 x 13 pan. Sprinkle with topping.
Bake 45 minutes in 350 degree oven.

Topping:

¼ cup granulated sugar
½ cup chopped nuts

½ cup shredded coconut
1 teaspoon cinnamon

This cake is real crunchy and simple to make. It doesn't take long to stir up. Can be served with whipped cream or ice cream.

* * * * *

RUM CAKE

From Linda

Cake:

6 eggs, separated
6 tablespoons flour
6 tablespoons sugar
¼ tablespoon baking powder

Beat the sugar and the egg-yolks for about 5 minutes.   Then add the flour and the baking powder one spoon at a time. Add a little rum to get a good consistency.

Beat the egg whites; fold into the above mixture and spoon into a square loaf pan (greased or lined with wax paper). Bake for approximately 30 minutes at 300 degrees.

Cool cake overnight and cut into three layers. Sprinkle the cake with rum. Spread jam or marmalade on one layer (typically the bottom layer.) Frost the other layers and the sides. Decorate with nuts or chocolate shavings.

Rum icing:

¼ pound butter
1 egg
½ cup powdered sugar

2 teaspoons potato flour or starch
2-3 teaspoons cocoa
3-4 tablespoons rum

Mix soft butter with eggs very well for approximately 2-3 minutes. Then add some of the sugar, cocoa, flour and mix. Then add some of the rum. Continue adding alternately until all is mixed and icing is smooth.

Note: As an alternative choice, you can frost bottom two layers and top with cherry sauce and whipped cream.

* * * * *

SAVANNAH TOFFEE TORT

Girl Scout Cookie Recipe

1 box Savannah cookies, rolled
½ cup chopped nutmeats
¼ pound butter
1 cup powdered sugar

1½ squares baking chocolate
3 eggs
pinch of salt

Cream butter and sugar. Add beaten egg yolks. Melt chocolate and add to above with salt. Fold in stiffly beaten egg whites. Grease 8 x 8 x 1 inch pan. Sprinkle half of cookie crumbs and nuts on bottom. Pour in mixture. Then sprinkle on the other half. Refrigerate for 12 hours before serving.

* * * * *

SOUR CREAM CAKE

1 cup sugar
2 eggs
1 cup sour cream
½ teaspoon soda

1 teaspoon baking powder
½ teaspoon salt
1 teaspoon lemon flavoring
1¾ cup flour

Beat sugar and eggs until very light, add the flavoring. Stir soda in sour cream and add alternately to the egg mixture with the flour mixed and sifted with the salt and baking powder. Bake in layers or as a loaf cake.

* * * * *

SPICE CAKE

1 cup butter
1½ cups sugar
3 cups sifted flour
3 eggs beaten separately
1 cup milk
1 teaspoon cinnamon

1½ teaspoons nutmeg
1 teaspoon vanilla
2 teaspoons baking powder
1 teaspoon ground cloves
1½ cups raisins

* * * * *

SUMMER SPECIAL POUND CAKE

Wi State Journal, June 6, 1965

¾ cup butter
1½ cups sugar
½ teaspoon almond extract
½ teaspoon vanilla
3 eggs

2½ cups sifted cake flour
1½ teaspoons baking powder
½ teaspoon salt
½ cup milk

Butter and lightly flour 7 cup mold; set aside. In mixing bowl cream together butter and sugar; blend in almond extract and vanilla. Add eggs, one at a time, beating well after each addition. Sift together flour, baking powder and salt. Add alternately with milk, beginning and ending with dry ingredients. Pour into mold and bake in a moderate (325 degree) oven for 1 hour and 35-40 minutes. Cool in mold for five minutes before removing to wire rack. Serves 10 – 12 people.

* * * * *

★ UP-SIDE DOWN CAKE

From Helen Schmoldt

2 tablespoons butter
1 cup brown sugar
1 cup canned cherries
4 tablespoons broken walnuts
2 eggs
1 cup sugar

1 cup flour
½ teaspoon salt
1 teaspoon baking powder
¼ cup water
½ teaspoon vanilla
½ cup whipping cream

Melt butter in frying pan; add brown sugar making a smooth layer. Cover evenly with cherries and sprinkle cherries with nuts. (Pour the following batter on top).

Beat yolks of eggs until thick and lemon color. Beating in sugar gradually. Mix and sift flour, salt and baking powder. Stir into first mixture. Add water and then vanilla and when mixture is smooth, fold in dry, stiffly beaten egg whites. Bake 40 minutes in a moderate oven with the most heat at the bottom. The brown sugar must melt and form a syrup. Turn cake out – upside down and cover with whipped cream.

* * * * *

 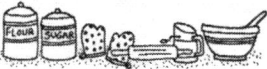 

★ WATERGATE CAKE

1 large package white cake mix
1 package pistachio pudding
3 eggs

1 cup oil
1 cup club soda or 7-up
½ cup nutmeats

Combine all ingredients except nuts. Mix 4 minutes. Add nuts. Bake 350 degrees for 35 – 40 minutes in a 9 x 13 pan.

Frosting:

1 package pistachio pudding
1½ cup milk

Beat pudding mix for 2 minutes. Fold in one large bowl of Cool Whip and spread on cake.

★ ★ ★ ★ ★

ZUCCHINI CAKE

Cream together:
3 eggs beat a little with spoon
1 cup oil

2 cups sugar
1 teaspoon vanilla

In another bowl
2 cups flour
2 teaspoons baking soda
1 teaspoon salt

1 teaspoon baking powder
3 teaspoons cinnamon

Make well, put liquid in. Add 2 cups shredded raw zucchini.

Grease and flour pan (9 x 13), bake at 350 degrees for 45 minutes.

★ ★ ★ ★ ★

Chocolate Cakes

BEST CHOCOLATE CAKE

2 cups cake flour
2 cups sugar
1 teaspoon baking soda
1 teaspoon salt
½ teaspoon baking powder
¾ cup water

¾ cup buttermilk
½ cup shortening
2 eggs
1 teaspoon vanilla
4 squares (1 oz ea) unsweetened chocolate melted and cooled

Heat oven to 350 degrees. Grease and flour 13 x 9 cake pan. Beat all ingredients in large mixer bowl on low speed, scraping bowl constantly, 30 seconds. Beat on high speed, scraping bowl occasionally 3 minutes. Pour into pan. Bake until wooden pick comes out clean, 50 to 55 minutes. Cool 10 minutes; remove from pan. Cool completely. Sprinkle with powdered sugar if desired.

* * * * *

CALUMET CHOCOLATE CAKE

From Mrs. Rote

¾ cup shortening
1¼ cups sugar
2½ teaspoons baking powder
1/8 teaspoon salt

2½ cups flour
¾ cup milk
4 eggs

Cream shortening, add sugar, and then add well beaten egg yolks. Mix and sift dry ingredients and add alternately with milk to first mixture. ½ teaspoon vanilla may be added. Fold in beaten egg whites. Pour into greased tins and bake in a moderate oven (325 – 350 degrees) for 30 minutes.

Chocolate Frosting

3½ squares unsweetened chocolate
2 cups powdered sugar
1 teaspoon vanilla

5 tablespoons milk
2 eggs yolks

Melt chocolate over hot water, add ½ the sugar, add milk, add remaining sugar and add yolk of eggs then cook in double boiler until thickens stirring constantly at first that the mixture may be perfectly smooth. Cool slightly, flavor and spread.

* * * * *

CHOCOLATE MINTED LIGHT CAKE

1 dozen Girl Scout Thin Mint cookies, crushed to medium fineness.
1 white cake mix.

Follow directions on cake mix box, folding in crushed Thin Mint crumbs just before putting cake in pan (or pans). Bake as directed. Frost using either white or chocolate frosting.

* * * * *

GERMAN'S CHOCOLATE CAKE

1 package Bakers German's Sweet
    Chocolate
½ cup boiling water
1 cup butter (or use margarine or other
    shortening)
2 cups sugar
4 egg yolks, unbeaten

1 teaspoon vanilla
½ teaspoon salt
1 teaspoon soda
2½ cups sifted cake flour
1 cup buttermilk
4 egg whites

Melt chocolate in ½ cup boiling water. Cool. Cream butter and sugar until light and fluffy. Add egg yolks, one at a time, and beat well after each. Add the melted chocolate and vanilla.

Sift together the salt, soda, and flour. Then add alternately with buttermilk to chocolate mixture, beating well. Beat until batter is smooth. Beat egg whites until stiff peaks form. Fold into batter. Pour into three 8 or 9 inch layer cake pans, line bottoms with paper. Bake in moderate oven (350 degrees) 35 – 40 minutes. Cool. Frost tops only with Coconut-Pecan Frosting, or use any favorite frosting or whipped cream.

Coconut-Pecan Frosting

Combine in saucepan:
1 cup of evaporated milk
1 cup of sugar
3 egg yolks

¼ pound margarine
1 teaspoon vanilla

Cook and stir over medium heat until mixture thickens (takes about 12 minutes.)

Add about 1 1/3 cups coconut and 1 cup of chopped pecans. Beat until frosting is cool and thick enough to spread. Makes 2 2/3 cups.

* * * * *

VELVETY CHOCOLATE CAKE

¼ cup milk
2 tablespoons white vinegar
2 cups all-purpose flour (unsifted)
½ cup cocoa (unsweetened)
1¼ teaspoons baking soda
1 teaspoon baking powder

½ teaspoon salt
¾ cup butter or margarine, softened
1 teaspoon vanilla extract
1½ cups sugar
2 eggs

Preheat oven to 350 degrees. Grease and lightly four two 9 inch round cake pans. Combine milk and vinegar; set aside for 10 minutes. In a small bowl place flour, cocoa, baking soda, baking powder and salt; mix thoroughly.

In a large bowl cream together butter and vanilla extract; gradually add sugar. Add eggs; beat until smooth. Add flour mixture alternately with milk mixture; beat until smooth. Pour into prepared pans. Bake until a cake tester inserted in center comes out clean, about 30 minutes. Cool in pans for 10 minutes. Remove from pans and place on wire racks to cool completely. Fill and frost cake with Delicate Seven Minutes Frosting.

* * * * *

Lemon Cakes

LEMON – LIME REFRIGERATOR SHEET CAKE

1 package lime gelatin (4 serving size)
1 package Duncan Hines Deluxe II Lemon Supreme Cake Mix

Topping:
1 envelope whipped topping mix (2 – 2½ cup yield)
1 package lemon instant pudding mix (4 serving size)
1½ cup cold milk

Dissolve gelatin in ¾ cup boiling water. Add ½ cup cold water; set aside at room temperature. Mix and bake cake as directed in a 13 x 9 x 2 inch pan. Cool cake 20 – 25 minutes. Poke deep holes through top of warm cake (still in pan) with meat fork or toothpick; space holes about one inch apart. With a cup, slowly pour gelatin mixture into holes. Refrigerate cake while preparing topping.

Topping:

In a chilled, deep bowl, blend and whip topping mix, instant pudding and cold milk until stiff (3 – 8 minutes). Immediately frost cake. Cake must be stored in refrigerator and served chilled. Frosted cake may be frozen for storage.

* * * * *

LEMON SUPREME POUND CAKE

1 package Duncan Hines Deluxe II Lemon Supreme Cake Mix
1 package lemon instant pudding mix (4 serving size)
½ cup oil
1 cup water
4 eggs

Preheat oven to 350 degrees. Blend all ingredients in a large bowl; beat at medium speed for 2 minutes. Bake in a greased and floured 10-inch tube pan at 350 degrees for 45 – 55 minutes, until center springs back when touched lightly. Cool right side up for about 25 minutes, then remove from pan.

Glaze: Blend 1 cup confectioners sugar with either 2 tablespoons milk OR 2 tablespoons lemon juice. Drizzle over cake.

* * * * *

LEMON SUPREME STREUSEL CAKE

1 package Duncan Hines Deluxe II Lemon Supreme Cake Mix
1 package lemon instant pudding mix (4 serving size)
2 tablespoons Crisco Oil
1 1/3 cups water
2 eggs

Preheat oven to 375 degrees. In large bowl, blend cake ingredients. Beat 2 minutes at medium speed. Do not over mix. Spread 3/4 of batter in greased and floured 10 inch tube pan. Combine streusel ingredients; sprinkle 2/3 cup over batter in pan. Spread remaining batter over streusel; top with reserved streusel. Bake 40 – 50 minutes. Cool right side up 25 minutes. Remove from pan and glaze top side up.

Streusel

½ cup flour
½ cup confectioner's sugar
2 tablespoons butter or margarine, melted

1 teaspoon lemon extract
3 drops yellow food coloring

Glaze

Combine 1 tablespoon water, 3 drops yellow food coloring, ¼ teaspoon lemon extract, and ¾ cup confectioner's sugar. Drizzle over cake.

* * * * *

TEXAS LEMON NUT CAKE

2 cups sugar
1 pound butter
6 eggs
3 ounces pure lemon extract
4 cups cake flour, separated

1 teaspoon baking powder
1 pound coarsely chopped pecans
1 pound halved brandied cherries
1 pound candied pineapple pieces

Cream sugar and butter together. One at a time beat in eggs. Add lemon extract. Add 3 cups sifted cake flour with baking powder.

To pecans, cherries, and pineapple add 1 cup cake flour and mix well. Mix all ingredients and put in two greased bread tins. Bake in a moderate oven (275 degrees F.) one hour and 45 minutes.

Yield: about 40 thin slices
Note: This recipe freezes well.

* * * * *

FROSTING

BUTTER FROSTING

1 tablespoon butter
½ cup powdered sugar
¾ tablespoon cream
½ teaspoon vanilla

* * * * *

EASY WHITE FROSING

Thicken 1 cup milk with 4 tablespoons flour
Let cool. Cream together:
1 cup vegetable shortening
1 cup white sugar
¼ teaspoon salt
1 teaspoon vanilla
Add cooled milk mixture and beat until fluffy.

* * * * *

DESSERT

★ APPLE CRISP

From Pauline Stauffacher

Apples – sliced
¼ + cup sugar
few cinnamon candies

Mix together until crumb mixture:
1 cup sugar
1 cup flour
1 teaspoon baking powder
pinch salt
1 egg

Put crumb mixture over apples.
Melt 1/3 cup butter and spoon over crumb mixture.
Sprinkle with cinnamon.

Bake 350 degrees for 1 hour.

★ ★ ★ ★ ★

APPLE CHERRY CRISP

From Jean

3 or 4 large cooking apples, sliced
2 or 3 cups sour cherries, pitted
½ teaspoon cinnamon
½ cup water or juice
1 teaspoon grated lemon rind

1 cup sugar
1 cup flour
scant pinch salt
½ cup butter

Arrange apple slices and cherries in shallow buttered baking dish. Sprinkle with cinnamon and water and lemon rind. Spread topping over fruit and bake at 350 degrees until browned and apples are tender. About 35 – 45 minutes. Serve warm with sour cream on the side.

Note: This dish is good with canned apples and cherries when fresh fruit is not available, or you can combine apples with half as many fresh cranberries at holiday times.

★ ★ ★ ★ ★

APPLE DESERT WITH WHEAT GERM

1 egg
¾ cup sugar
1½ cup chopped pared apples
½ cup wheat germ
½ cup flour

1 teaspoon baking powder
¾ teaspoon cinnamon
¼ teaspoon salt
1/8 teaspoon nutmeg

Serve with either whipped cream or ice cream

★ ★ ★ ★ ★

86

AVOCADO DESSERT

From Prevention

2 peeled, ripe avocados
2 bananas
1 cup seedless grapes
1 cup yogurt
2 tablespoons honey

3 tablespoons fresh orange juice
2 teaspoons grated lemon rind
1 tablespoon fresh lemon juice
1/8 teaspoon sea salt

Chop the avocados and bananas into bite sized pieces and combine with grapes. Beat yogurt for about 1 minute and stir in the honey, orange juice, lemon juice, lemon rind and sea salt. Pour this sauce over the fruit mixture and serve immediately.

* * * * *

BLUEBERRY TORTE

From Mrs. Steve Walden

2 cups graham cracker crumbs (about 20 crackers)
½ cup butter, melted
½ cup brown sugar (packed)
1 (8-oz) package cream cheese

½ cup granulated sugar
2 eggs
2 tablespoons lemon juice
1 (No. 2) can blueberry pie filling

Mix crumbs, butter and brown sugar. Pat into a 9 x 9 inch pan. Mix cream cheese and granulated sugar until smooth. Add eggs, one at a time, beating them. Add lemon juice. Pour over crumbs in pan. Bake 20 minutes. Top with blueberries when cool. Serve with cream.

* * * * *

★ BRATZLIE

From Wilma

1 pound butter (soft)
Cream into the butter:
1 cup white sugar
1 cup brown sugar

Add:
6 eggs
½ lemon
¼ cup rich milk or cream (can use half and half)
Add:

5 cups flour
½ teaspoon cinnamon
1 teaspoon salt
1 teaspoon vanilla

Store in refrigerator overnight. In morning take out and make into balls.

Divide dough in half before forming balls.

* * * * *

★ BRATZLI

From Rose Voelkli

Very good

¾ cup butter
¾ cup vegetable shortening
4 eggs
1 cup light brown sugar
1 cup white sugar

1 teaspoon salt
½ teaspoon cinnamon
1 teaspoon lemon extract
grated rind of 1 lemon
4 cups flour

Cream the butter and shortening thoroughly. Add the brown sugar and cream again. Beat the eggs well. Add white sugar and beat again. Combine the two mixtures, and add the 4 cups flour. Chill several hours. Make it into balls the size of hickory nuts. Place the balls of dough upon a special bratzeli iron. Form and bake according to directions of iron.

★ ★ ★ ★ ★

BUTTERFINGER DESSERT

1 angel food cake
6 Butterfinger candy bars
1 pint cream, whipped
½ cup soft butter

2 cups powdered sugar
4 egg yolks
2 teaspoons vanilla

Beat butter, sugar, egg yolks and vanilla until thick. Fold in whipped cream. Break one-half of the cake into a loaf pan; pour one half of the custard over the cake. Break three candy bars over custard. Repeat with cake, custard, ending with candy bars. Refrigerate overnight. Serve next day.

★ ★ ★ ★ ★

CHERRY DESSERT

From Mrs. Allen Zeal, Monroe, WI

Crush 21 graham crackers
Add ½ cup soft butter
½ cup sugar
Mix well.

Line 9 x 13 greased pan with crumbs.

Then cream well
1 large package cream cheese
2 eggs
½ cup sugar
1 teaspoon vanilla

Spread on crust and bake in 350 degree oven for about 20-25 minutes. Don't over bake. Cool.

When cool, cover with 2 cans of cherry pie filling. When you are ready to eat, add a little whipped cream to each dish.

Whipped Cream

½ cup whipping cream
¼ cup sugar
a little vanilla.

* * * * *

DOUBLE CHERRY DESSERT

1 package Cherry Chip cake mix
2 eggs
½ cup butter or margarine, melted
1 can (21 oz) cherry pie filling
½ cup chopped walnuts or pecans (optional)
Glaze

Heat oven to 350 degrees. Mix cake mix (dry), eggs and butter until smooth. Spread dough in ungreased oblong pan (13 x 2). Spread pie filling over dough; sprinkle with nuts. Bake 40 – 45 minutes. Cool 15 minutes; drizzle with Glaze. Serve warm or cool. 12 – 15 servings.

Glaze:

Mix 1 cup confectioner's sugar and 1 tablespoon water. Add enough additional water (1 – 2 teaspoons) to reach desired glaze consistency.

* * * * *

FROSTED PRETZELS

2 boxes Nabisco Veri-Thin Mister Salty pretzels (10 oz box)

2 pounds white almond bark.

* * * * *

FRUIT DESSERT

Crust:
Combine and pat into 9 x 13 pan:
21 graham crackers, crushed
½ cup melted butter
½ cup granulated sugar

Beat together:
1 (8-oz) package softened cream cheese
2 eggs
½ cup sugar
1 teaspoon vanilla

Put on top of graham cracker crumb mixture. Bake for 25 minutes at 350 degrees. Cool and spread either cherry or blueberry pie filling on top. May serve with whipped cream.

A combination of peach and blueberry pie filling may be used.

* * * * *

GOLDEN TASSIES

From Mr. Robert Putnam, Monroe

½ cup butter
1 (3 oz) pkg cream cheese
1 cup sifted flour

Cream softened butter and cream cheese. Mix in flour till blended. Pinch off a small amount and line small muffin tins; the thinner the better.

Filling:
Beat 2 eggs just enough to mix.
Add
1½ cups light brown sugar firmly packed
2 tablespoons melted butter
pinch of salt
½ teaspoon vanilla

Grind 1 cup pecans and place some pecans in shells, adding 1 teaspoon filling on nut meats, sprinkle nut meats over filling.

Bake at 350 degrees for 15 minutes then at 250 degrees for 10 minutes or until golden brown. Remove from pan immediately.

* * * * *

PINEAPPLE DESSERT

From Mrs. Wilbert Christen

¾ cup butter
1 (8 oz) pkg cream cheese
1¼ cups sifted powdered sugar
1 (No. 2) can crushed pineapple

1 (12 oz) pkg coconut bar cookies
2 (3-oz) pkgs cherry Jell-O
½ pint whipping cream (sweetened)

Beat butter, cream cheese, and powdered sugar until fluffy. Fold in drained pineapple. (Save juice.) Butter 9 x 13 inch pan and line with coconut bars (do not crush). Spread one-half of pineapple mixture over cookies. Add another layer of uncrushed cookies and spread on rest of pineapple mixture.

Put in refrigerator and let set.

Dissolve Jell-O using pineapple juice and enough boiling water to make 2 cups. Add 2 cups cold water, chill until slightly thickened. Beat until fluffy and pour over cookie-pineapple layers.

Frost with whipped cream when Jell-O is set, or just before server. Serves 12.

* * * * *

PISTACHIO-CREAM ECLAIRS

From Good Housekeeping

1 cup water
½ cup butter or margarine
¼ teaspoon salt
1 cup all-purpose flour
4 eggs

1 (3 5/8 oz) or (3 ¾ oz) pkg pistachio instant pudding mix
1 cup heavy or whipping cream, whipped
Choc Glaze

1. Prepare éclair shells:
    Preheat oven to 375 degrees. Grease a large cookie sheet. In 2 quart saucepan over medium heat, heat water, butter and salt until butter melts and mixture boils. Reduce heat to low. With a wooden spoon vigorously stir in flour until mixture forms a ball and leaves side of pan. Remove from heat. Let cool a minute or two.
2. Beat eggs into mixture until thoroughly blended. Drop mixture by ¼ cupful onto cookie sheet 2 inches apart. With small spatula, spread each mound of mixture into 5 x ¾ inch rectangles rounding edges. Bake 40 minutes or until lightly browned. Cut a slit in side of each and bake 10 minutes longer. Cool shells on wire racks.
3. Meanwhile prepare pudding mix as label directs but use only 1 cup milk. With rubber spatula, fold in whipped cream, refrigerate.
4. Prepare Choc Glaze. Slice about 1/3 from top of each shell and fill bottom of shells with pudding mixture, replace top. Spread glaze on top of éclairs.

Choc Glaze:

In 1 cup glass measuring cup place
½ cup semi-sweet chocolate pieces
1 tablespoon butter or margarine
1½ teaspoon milk
1½ teaspoons light corn syrup.

In 1 quart saucepan over low heat in 1 inch hot, not boiling water, place measuring cup and heat chocolate mixture until chocolate is melted and smooth, stirring occasionally.

* * * * *

POP-OVERS THAT POP

From Mrs. Rote

1 cup flour
¼ teaspoon salt
1 cup milk
2 eggs, beaten
1 tablespoon Crisco or lard, melted

Sift flour and salt. Add milk gradually, then eggs and Crisco. Beat batter 5 minutes with egg beater. Pour into hot Crisco muffin pans or other cups. Bake in hot oven (400 degrees) for 30 minutes. Do not open oven door while baking. This recipe makes 10.

* * * * *

PUDDING NUT TORTE

From Irene Riesen 3/6/79

Very Good

Crust:
1 cup flour
½ cup butter or margarine
½ cup chopped nuts

Press into 9 x 13 greased pan. Bake 15 minutes at 350 degrees, and then cool.

Beat until fluffy:
1 cup cool whip
1 (8-oz) package cream cheese
1 cup powdered sugar

Spread this on crust.
Whip:
1 large package instant pudding *
3 cups milk

Put on top of second layer.

Top with:
1 cup cool whip
1 cup chopped nuts

Refrigerate.
* You can use chocolate, butterscotch or lemon pudding

* * * * *

RITZ CRACKER DESSERT

Mary Chmid

18 Ritz crackers – crushed
Beat 4 egg whites stiff
Add 1 cup sugar gradually

Fold in:
1 teaspoon baking powder
1 teaspoon vanilla
½ cup chopped pecans
Add cracker crumbs

Put into buttered 9" pie tin and bake 35-40 minutes at 325 degrees.
Serve cold with whipped cream.

* * * * *

RHUBARB BUTTER CRUNCH

From Mrs.Marvin Malkow

Combine:
3 cups diced fresh rhubarb
1 cup sugar
3 tablespoons flour
Place in greased 6x10 pan.

Combine:
1 cup brown sugar
1 cup rolled oats
1½ cup flour
Cut in 1 cup butter.

Sprinkle over rhubarb. Bake at 375 degrees 40 minutes.
Serve with cream or ice cream.

* * * * *

★ RHUBARB CRISP

From Jean

Put in baking dish:
3 cups rhubarb
1 cup sugar
3 tablespoon flour

Mix until crumbly and sprinkle over rhubarb mixture:
1 cup brown sugar
1 cup quick oatmeal
1½ cup flour
½ cup butter or shortening

* * * * *

ROSETTE'S

Editor's Note: This is the recipe Granny gave me.
Mix Batter:

Sift together 1 cup sifted flour, ½ teaspoon salt, 1 tablespoon sugar. Gradually stir into a mixture of 2 slightly beaten eggs, 1 cup milk and 1 tablespoon salad oil. Beating only until smooth. Strain and let stand an hour if full of air bubbles.

Heat Iron

Set iron in pan of deep fat and heat to 370 degrees or until an inch cube of bread browns in 1 minute. Drain iron slightly on unglazed paper and dip into batter, covering only the bottom and sides of the iron to about 1/8 inch of the top.

Fry and Drain

Lower iron into fat and fry 1 – 1 ½ minutes or until delicately browned. Remove from fat, loosen from iron with a fork and place on unglazed paper; invert to drain inside. If fat is too hot or cold, the batter will not cling to the iron.

Serve on a Tray

Dusted with confectioner's sugar, rosettes are a nice addition to the tea table. They become fork food when topped with a dessert sauce, fresh or stewed fruit, ice cream or whipped cream flavored with jam.

Recipe yields approximately 40 rosettes.

* * * * *

STRAWBERRY DESSERT

From Mrs. Delbert Kundert

First layer:
1 cup flour
¼ cup brown sugar
½ cup butter
¾ cup chopped nuts.

Mix and put in 9 x 13 pan. Bake at 350 degrees for 15 minutes.

Second layer:
24 marshmallows
2/3 cup milk

Heat together in double boiler until marshmallows melt.
Cool. Then fold marshmallow mixture into:
1 cup cream – whipped

Spread on first layer. Refrigerate until set.

Third layer:
2 packages strawberry Jell-O
Dissolve in
2 cups boiling water
Add
1 package frozen strawberries

When slightly thickened, pour mixture over the other layers. Refrigerate overnight or several hours. (Other Jell-O flavors may be substituted.)

* * * * *

VEGETABLE-FRUIT DESSERT ICES

From Miss Sorah Shapiro, Brooklyn, NY (Prevention)

A great substitute for ices or ice cream, it's rich in vitamins – and no sugar.

1 quart fresh carrot juice
3 large oranges
3 medium bananas
3 tablespoons honey (if desired)

Put all ingredients into blender and mix at high speed until very smooth. Pour into ice-cube trays and freeze. For smoother consistency re-blend and refreeze. Place in lower portion of refrigerator an hour before serving.

* * * * *

94

WHEAT GERM APPLE CRISP

From Good Housekeeping Magazine

6 cups sliced, peeled and cored cooking apples (about 6 medium apples)
2/3 cup packed brown sugar
½ cup all-purpose flour
1/3 cup toasted wheat germ with sugar and honey
6 tablespoons butter or margarine (softened)

Grease shallow 1½ quart casserole. Place apple slices in casserole. In medium bowl, mix remaining ingredients thoroughly. Sprinkle over apples. Bake in 375 degree oven for 45 minutes or until apples are tender. Serve warm. Makes 6 servings.

* * * * *

  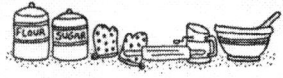

Cookies

ANGEL WHISPERS

Good

1 cup butter or margarine
½ cup sifted confectioner's sugar
1 teaspoon lemon extract

2 cups sifted all-purpose flour
¼ teaspoon salt
Lemon filling

Cream butter to consistency of mayonnaise. Add sugar gradually while continuing to cream. Add remaining ingredients (except filling); blend well. Chill. Measure level teaspoons of dough, round into ball then flatten slightly. Place about 1 inch apart on ungreased baking sheet. Bake at 400 degrees for 8 – 10 minutes or until edges are lightly browned. Put together with Lemon Filling. Makes about 5 dozen double cookies.

Lemon Filling

1 egg, slightly beaten
Grated peel of 1 lemon
2/3 cup sugar

3 tablespoons lemon juice
1½ tablespoons soft butter or margarine

Blend all ingredients in top of double boiler. Cook over hot water, stirring constantly until thick. Chill until firm.

* * * * *

APPLE-SEED COOKIES

It's always nice to have good nutritional cookies on hand for the children.

1 cup grated apple (tart)
1 egg
2 tablespoons safflower oil
2 tablespoons honey

pinch sea salt
¾ cup raisins
¾ cup sunflower seed meal
(sesame meal to sprinkle tops of cookies)

Mix egg, oil, honey and apple together. Add remaining ingredients. Spoon-drop on oiled cookie sheet. Bake about 15-20 minutes in moderate oven.

* * * * *

AUNT BELL'S GINGER COOKIES

From Mrs. Jo Rice

Boil:
1 cup molasses
1 cup sugar

1 cup butter or butter & lard
8 tablespoons boiling water
2 teaspoons soda
1 teaspoon ginger
½ teaspoon cinnamon
½ teaspoon cloves
Have molasses cold
Flour and roll out and back in quick oven.

* * * * *

BITS 'O BRICKLE COOKIES

1 cup brown sugar
1 cup white sugar
1 cup butter or margarine
½ teaspoon salt
3 eggs, beaten

2 teaspoons soda
2 teaspoons cream of tartar
3½ cups flour
1 teaspoon vanilla
1 bag Bits 'O Brickle

Mix all ingredients in order given. Roll in small (walnut-sized) balls. Place on greased cookie sheets. Flatten with sugar-dipped glass bottom. Bake at 350 degrees until a light brown. About 10 – 12 minutes.

* * * * *

BROWN SUGAR COOKIES

From Helen Schmoldt

1½ cups brown sugar
¾ cup butter
¼ cup water
1 teaspoon soda

1 cup raisins
1 cup walnuts
2½ cups flour
2 eggs, well beaten

Cream butter and sugar. Add beaten eggs, and mix. Sift soda with flour. Add to first mixture. Add water, raisins and nuts. Drop from spoon onto pan and bake in moderate oven (350 degrees.)

* * * * *

BUTTER COOKIES

Cream well
1 cup butter
1 cup sugar

Add
1 egg
1 teaspoon vanilla

Sift together
½ teaspoon soda
½ teaspoon salt
2 cups flour

Bake at 375 degrees.
Makes about 60-70 cookies

* * * * *

BUTTER CREAM COOKIES

From Mrs. Sylvester Granberg, Monroe, WI

½ cup butter
1½ cups brown sugar
1 cup sour cream
½ teaspoon soda
2 eggs

1 teaspoon vanilla
½ teaspoon baking powder
½ teaspoon salt
2/3 cup nuts
2¾ cups flour

Cream butter, sugar, add eggs and beat. Add sour cream, vanilla. Sift dry ingredients and add to first mixture. Add nuts. Chill 1 hour. Drop by teaspoons about 2 inches apart on greased cookie sheet. Bake at 375 degrees about 8 – 10 minutes.

Frost with:
½ cup powdered sugar
few drops of vanilla
2 – 3 tablespoons milk or cream

* * * * *

BUTTERNUT DROPS

Christmas Cookie

½ cup butter
¼ cup sugar
1 egg, separated
½ teaspoon vanilla
¼ teaspoon salt
1 cup cake flour

1 tablespoon lemon juice
2 tablespoons granted orange rind
1 tablespoon grated lemon rind
½ cup Brazil nuts, ground fine
candied cherries

Cream butter and sugar well. Add egg yolk and flavoring. Beat well. Sift dry ingredients together and add with lemon juice and rinds. Mix thoroughly and place in covered bowl. Chill. Roll into tiny balls [½ teaspoon of dough per ball.] Dip balls into slightly beaten egg white. Roll in ground nuts. Place on greased cookie sheet. Press ½ candied cherry on top of each and bake at 350 degrees for 25 minutes.

Makes 40 cookies.

* * * * *

BUTTERSCOTCH DANDIES

2 (6 oz) pkg (2 cups) butterscotch chips
1 (3 oz) can (2 cups) chow mein noodles
1 (7 oz) can (1 ½ cup) salted peanuts

Melt chips over hot water (not boiling). Place noodles and peanuts in bowl. Add melted chips and stir until well blended. Drop by rounded teaspoonful on aluminum foil lined cookie sheet. Chill till firm.

Yield: About 4 dozen

* * * * *

BUTTERSCOTCH REFRIGERATOR COOKIES

1 (6 oz) pkg butterscotch pieces
½ cup (1 stick) butter
2/3 cup firmly packed light brown sugar
1 egg
1½ cup regular all-purpose flour
¾ teaspoon baking soda
1/3 cup chopped nuts
1/3 cup raisins, optional

In a small double boiler or in a heavy saucepan over low heat, melt butterscotch pieces. In mixing bowl cream butter; gradually add sugar and beat until light and fluffy. Beat in egg; then beat in melted butterscotch. Sift together flour and baking soda; gradually add to creamed mixture. Blend in nuts and raisins, if desired. Chill for ease in handling. On waxed paper shape into 2 rolls, each 10 inches long and 1¼ inch in diameter. Wrap in waxed paper; chill several hours or overnight. Cut rolls into ¼ inch slices and place on baking sheet. Bake in preheated 375 degree oven 8 – 10 minutes. Let cool about 1 minute; remove from baking sheets to wire rack to cool.
Yield: Approximately 4 dozen refrigerator cookies.

* * * * *

CAROL'S OATMEAL COOKIES

From Mrs. Edward Riese

Buttered baking sheets
Yield: 4 – 5 dozen
Preheated 400 degree oven

2½ cups sifted all-purpose flour
½ teaspoon salt
2 teaspoons cinnamon
½ teaspoon nutmeg
½ teaspoon cloves
1 teaspoon soda
1 cup (2 sticks) butter, softened

2 cups firmly packed brown sugar
2 eggs, lightly beaten
1 cup sour cream
2 cups oatmeal (either quick cook or regular)
2 cups chopped dates
1 cup chopped nuts

Sift together first six ingredients; set aside. Cream butter and sugar, add eggs; mix well. Add sour cream and mix thoroughly. Stir in dry ingredients. Add oatmeal, fruit and nuts. Mix well. Drop by teaspoons onto cookie sheets. Bake 12 – 15 minutes.

NOTE: A combination of raisins and figs may be substituted for dates.

* * * * *

CHERRY PINWHEELS

Refrigerator Cookies

1 cup sugar
1 cup butter
2 eggs, beaten
½ teaspoon almond extract

3 cups sifted all-purpose flour
2 teaspoons baking powder
½ teaspoon salt

Cream sugar and butter until fluffy. Beat in eggs and extract. Blend in sifted dry ingredients. Chill dough. Roll one-half of dough to 8 x 12 inch rectangle. Spread with one-half of Cherry Filling. Roll up, beginning with wide side as for jell roll. Wrap and chill. Repeat process for remaining dough. Slice and bake on greased baking sheet in moderate oven (375 degrees) for 8 – 10 minutes. Makes 6 dozen.

CHERRY FILLING: Drain 2 jars (8 oz size) maraschino cherries, reserving 1 cup of liquid. Thicken liquid with 2 tablespoons cornstarch, stirring constantly over low heat. Remove from heat. Add ¼ teaspoon salt; drained cherries, finely cut; and 2 cups ground blanched almonds. Cool.

* * * * *

★ CHERUB COINS

From Parade's Test Kitchen

Very Good (One of Granny's Christmas traditions)

¾ cup butter or margarine
1 ½ cup firmly packed light-brown sugar
1 egg, unbeaten
2 cups sifted cake flour

1/8 teaspoon baking soda
½ teaspoon salt
¼ cup finely chopped pecans

Cream butter or margarine and sugar; add egg, mix well. Mix and sift flour, baking soda and salt. Add gradually. Mix well after each addition. Stir in chopped pecans. Chill overnight. Shape into tiny balls ½ inch in diameter. Place on greased cookie sheets; flatten slightly with thumb. Bake at 375 degrees for 8 – 10 minutes. Let stand a few minutes before removing from cookie sheets. Makes about 10 dozen cookies.

* * * * *

CRISP FLAKE COOKIES

1 ¼ cup sifted Swans Down Cake Flour
½ teaspoon baking powder
½ teaspoon salt
½ teaspoon baking soda
1/3 cup butter

½ cup granulated sugar
½ cup firmly packed brown sugar
1 egg
1 teaspoon vanilla
1 cup Post 40% Bran Flakes

Mix flour, baking powder, salt and soda. Cream butter. Gradually add sugars and continue creaming until light and fluffy. Add egg and vanilla; beat well. Add flour mixture and cereal, mixing just until blended.

Drop by teaspoon onto ungreased baking sheets. Bake at 375 degrees for 10 – 12 minutes or until golden brown. Cool slightly. Remove from baking sheets. Store in tightly covered container. Makes about 2 dozen cookies.

Chocolate Chip Flake Cookies

Prepare Crisp Flake Cookies as directed, adding 1 package (6 oz) semi-sweet chocolate chips with the cereal. Makes about 2 ½ dozen cookies.

* * * * *

CHOCOLATE CHIP COOKIES

1 package Duncan Hines Deluxe II White Cake Mix
¼ cup light brown sugar
1 cup (6 oz) semi-sweet chocolate chips
½ cup chopped nuts
¾ cup oil
1 egg

Preheat oven to 375 degrees.

In a large bowl stir all ingredients together until well-mixed. Drop from a teaspoon onto an ungreased cookie sheet.

Bake at 375 degrees for 10 – 12 minutes, until centers of cookies are golden brown. (Edges will look darker.)

Cool on cookie sheet for about 1 minute. Then remove to rack to finish cooling.
Make about 3 ½ dozen 1 ½ inch cookies.

* * * * *

CHOCOLATE CHIP PUDDING COOKIES

2¼ cups unsifted all-purpose flour
1 teaspoon baking soda
1 cup butter or margarine, softened
¼ cup granulated sugar
¾ cup firmly packed light brown sugar

1 pkg (4-serving size) Jell-O instant pudding and pie filling *
1 teaspoon vanilla
2 eggs
1 (12 oz) pkg chocolate chips
1 cup chopped nuts (optional)

* Butter Pecan, Butterscotch, Chocolate, Milk Chocolate, Chocolate Fudge, French Vanilla or Vanilla Flavor pudding.

Mix flour with baking soda. Combine butter, the sugars, pudding mix and vanilla in large mixer bowl. Beat until smooth and creamy. Beat in eggs. Gradually add flour mixture. Then stir in chips and nuts. Batter will be stiff. Drop by rounded measuring teaspoonfuls onto ungreased baking sheets, about 2 inches apart. Bake at 375 degrees for 8 – 10 minutes. Makes about 7 dozen.

* * * * *

★ CHOCOLATE DROP COOKIES

From Helen Schmoldt

1 cup sugar
½ cup butter (fat)
2 eggs
2 squares melted chocolate
½ cup nutmeats

½ cup sour milk
1¾ cup flour
½ teaspoon soda
1 teaspoon vanilla
2½ teaspoons cinnamon

Cream butter and sugar; add beaten yolks and milk. Add flour sifted with soda, and then melted chocolate. Fold stiffly beaten egg whites into the batter. Then add nuts. Drop and bake in 350 degree oven. (Raisins can be added instead of nuts). Frost with Mocha Frosting.

* * * * *

CHOCOLATE ORANGE TEA DROPS

From Mrs. James Roth

½ cup soft butter
1 (3 oz) pkg cream cheese
½ cup sugar
1 egg
1 teaspoon grated orange rind

1 teaspoon vanilla
1 cup sifted flour
½ teaspoon salt
1 (6 oz) pkg semi-sweet chocolate pieces

Heat oven to 350 degrees (moderate). Mix butter, cream cheese, sugar, egg, orange rind and vanilla. Sift flour and salt together and stir in. Stir in chocolate pieces, mixing thoroughly. Drop teaspoonfuls about 1 inch apart onto lightly greased baking sheet. Bake about 15 minutes, until cookies are delicately browned at edges. Makes about 3 dozen cookies.

* * * * *

CHOCO-NUT CRUNCHIES

From Mrs. Ray Atkins, Kansas City, Kansas

Refrigerator Cookies

2 cups sifted all purpose flour
1 teaspoon baking powder
½ teaspoon salt
½ cup butter
1½ cups sugar

2 eggs
2 squares unsweetened chocolate, melted
1 teaspoon vanilla
1 cup chopped nuts

Sift together dry ingredients. Cream butter and sugar until fluffy. Add eggs and beat thoroughly. Blend in melted chocolate and vanilla. Stir in sifted dry ingredients and nuts. Pack cookie mixture into small refrigerator tray lined with wax paper. Chill overnight. Turn dough out of tray and slice 1/8 inch thick. Bake on greased baking sheet in moderate oven (375 degrees) for 12 – 15 minutes. Cool on rack. Make about 3 ½ dozen.

* * * * *

CHUNKY PEANUT BUTTER COOKIES

From Good Housekeeping Magazine

350 degree oven

2¼ cups all purpose flour
1 cup chunky peanut butter
2/3 cup honey
½ cup sugar

½ cup butter or margarine softened
2 eggs
½ teaspoon baking powder

Into large bowl, measure all ingredients. With mixer at low speed, beat ingredients until well mixed, occasionally scraping bowl. Drop batter by level tablespoons, 2 inches apart, onto cookie sheets. Bake 15 minutes or until lightly browned. With pancake turner, immediately remove cookies to wire racks. Cool. Store in tightly covered container. Makes about 2½ dozen cookies.

* * * * *

CONFETTI COOKIES

1 cup sugar
½ cup brown sugar
1 cup shortening
2 eggs
1 teaspoon vanilla

2 1/3 cups Robin Hood All purpose flour
1 teaspoon salt *
1 teaspoon soda *
1 cup cut-up small gum drops
½ cup chopped nuts

CREAM..... sugars, shortening, eggs and vanilla
SPOON..... unsifted flour into dry measuring cup
POUR...... measured flour onto a square of waxed paper
ADD........ salt and soda to flour (not sifted) and stir to blend
ADD........ blended dry ingredients to creamed mixture and mix well
STIR IN..... gum drops and nuts; mix well.
DROP....... by teaspoonfuls onto greased baking sheet. Dot tops with additional cut-up gum drops, if desired.
BAKE ...... at 350 degrees for 15 minutes
YIELD...... 5 – 6 dozen cookies
* If you use ROBIN HOOD Pre sifted Self-Rising flour (sold in some sections of the country) omit salt and soda.

* * * * *

CRANBERRY COCONUT JUMBLES

3 cups sifted flour
2 teaspoons baking powder
¼ teaspoon salt
1½ cups fresh cranberries, coarsely chopped
1 cup finely grated coconut

½ cup shortening
½ cup butter
1½ cups sugar
3 eggs, well beaten
1 tablespoon grated lemon peel
1 tablespoon lemon juice

Mix together and sift flour, baking powder, and salt. Stir in cranberries and coconut. Cream shortening and butter; gradually add sugar. Add eggs and beat well. Add lemon peel and juice; gradually stir in flour mixture. Drop from teaspoon onto lightly greased cookie sheet. Bake in a moderate oven (375 degrees) about 10 minutes, or until lightly browned.

Makes 5 dozen 2-inch cookies.

* * * * *

★ DATE COOKIES

From Mrs. Rote

½ cup butter
1½ cups brown sugar
2 eggs
1 cup sour milk
1 teaspoon soda

1 teaspoon baking powder
2½ – 3 cups flour
1 cup dates
½ cup nuts
1 teaspoon vanilla

Fold in beaten egg whites at last.

* * * * *

★DATE FILLED OATMEAL COOKIES

From Dottie

1 cup sugar
1 cup shortening (½ butter & ½ lard)
salt
2 cups flour

2 cups oatmeal
½ cup milk
½ teaspoon cinnamon
½ teaspoon soda dissolved in vinegar

Filling:
1 cup sugar
1 cup water
1 pound dates

* * * * *

★ DATE ROLL COOKIES

From Will Hartwig

2 cups brown sugar
1 cup shortening
2 eggs
1 tablespoon hot water

1 teaspoon soda in hot water
3½ cups flour
1 teaspoon baking powder

Mix shortening and sugar. Add eggs, soda and water, flour, and baking powder. Divide dough in two portions. Poll out to ¼ inch thickness. Spread with the filling and roll up in waxed paper, which prevents breaking, chill, slice and bake.

Filling:
1 cup chopped dates
½ cup water
½ cup sugar
Heat and cool.

* * * * *

FANCY HOLIDAY COOKIES – SANTAS WHISKERS

1 cup butter or margarine
1 cup sugar
2 tablespoons milk
1 teaspoon vanilla or rum
2½ cups sifted all purpose flour

¾ cup finely chopped red and green cherries
½ cup finely chopped pecans
¾ cup flaked coconut

In mixer bowl cream butter and sugar. Blend in milk and flavoring. Stir in flour, candied cherries and nuts. Form into 2 rolls, each 2 inches x 8 inches. Roll in coconut. Wrap and chill several hours or overnight. Slice into ¼ inch thick slices. Place on ungreased cookie sheet. Bake in 375 degree oven for 12 minutes or till edges are golden. Makes about 5 dozen cookies.

* * * * *

★ FILLED COOKIES

1/3 cup shortening
1 cup sugar
1 egg
½ cup milk

1 teaspoon vanilla
3½ cups flour
½ teaspoon salt
4 teaspoons baking powder

Cream shortening; add sugar, beaten eggs, milk and vanilla.
Add flour, salt and baking powder, which have been sifted together.
Roll out thin on slightly floured board and cut with cookie cutter.

Double Filling for this cookie recipe.
Date Filling
1 cup raisins
1 cup dates, cut fine
1 cup sugar

1 cup cold water
1 Tablespoon flour
½ cup chopped nuts.

Mix four and sugar. Boil all ingredients together until thick. Cool before placing between cookies.

* * * * *

FROSTED ORANGE COOKIES

Editor's Note: These are the cookies us grandkids looked for in the pantry.
Sift together:
3½ cups all purpose flour
1 teaspoon soda

1 teaspoon baking powder
¼ teaspoon salt

Cream thoroughly:
¾ cup butter
1½ cups sugar

3 eggs, beaten
4 tablespoons orange juice
Grated rind of 1 orange
1 cup buttermilk or sour cream

Add the beaten eggs, orange juice and rind to the creamed sugar and butter. Alternately add dry ingredients and buttermilk. Chill. Drop from teaspoon 2 inches apart on an ungreased cookie sheet. Bake in a 400 degree oven for about 15 minutes.

Frost with orange frosting made by adding orange juice to confectioners sugar to spreading consistency.

Makes 50 cookies. Cool before storing.

[Granny uses part butter and part shortening.]

* * * * *

GINGERSNAPS

1 cup brown sugar
1 cup molasses
1 cup butter (scant)

2 teaspoons ginger & 2 teaspoons soda in
3 tablespoons hot water
1 teaspoon cinnamon
(Flour)

Mix very stiff and roll thin and bake.

* * * * *

GRAHAM KISSES

2 cups coarsely crushed honey graham cracker crumbs. (about 10 double crackers)
1 cup chopped nuts
1 cup shredded coconut
3 egg whites
6 tablespoons sugar
½ teaspoon vanilla

Heat oven to hot (400 degrees). Combine graham cracker crumbs, nuts and coconut in a large mixing bowl. In another bowl, beat egg whites until stiff but not dry. Gradually add sugar, beating until a stiff meringue is formed. Stir in vanilla and crumb mixture. Drop from tablespoon onto greased cookie sheets. Bake for 20 – 25 minutes or until lightly browned and crisp to the touch. Remove to wire racks and cool. Makes about 24 cookies.

* * * * *

GRANOLA COOKIES

½ cup shortening
1 cup firmly packed brown sugar
1 egg
1 teaspoon vanilla
¼ cup milk

1 ¼ cup sifted flour
½ teaspoon soda
¼ teaspoon salt
2 cups granola *

Cream shortening and sugar, add remaining ingredients; mix well. Drop by teaspoonfuls onto greased cookie sheets. Bake in preheated moderate (350 degree) oven about 11 minutes.

Yield: 2½ dozen.
* See recipe for Basic Granola.

* * * * *

GREEN ANGEL DELIGHT

(Girl Scout Cookie Recipe)

1 (14 ½ oz) can evaporated milk (1 2/3 cup)
1 (3 oz) package lime gelatin
1 2/3 cups hot water
1 cup sugar
¼ cup lime juice

2 tablespoons lemon juice
2 cups crushed Girl Scout Sandwich Cookie crumbs
½ cup melted butter
chocolate bits

Mix butter with chocolate crumbs. Line shallow dish with mixture. Whip milk, which has been chilled in freezing compartment. Dissolve gelatin in hot water. After partially set, whip until fluffy. Add juice and sugar to gelatin. Fold in whipped milk and chocolate bits. Pour over cookie crumbs. Place in refrigerator until ready to serve.

* * * * *

HALF MOON COOKIES

½ cup butter
1 cup sugar
1 teaspoon vanilla
1 egg

2 squares melted chocolate or   4-5 teaspoons of cocoa
2 cups flour
½ teaspoon baking soda
1 teaspoon salt
¾ cup milk

Cream shortening, sugar, and vanilla together until fluffy. Beat in egg, then chocolate. Sift flour with baking soda and salt. Add to creamed mixture alternately with milk.

Bake on ungreased cookie sheet. Bake in 375 degree oven 10-12 minutes.

Cookies are cake like. Frost ½ cookie with melted sweet chocolate and the other ½ with confectioner's sugar. Make 3 dozen.

* * * * *

HALLOWEEN COOKIES

Raisin Happy Faces

½ cup butter
1 cup sugar
1 teaspoon grated orange peel
2 teaspoons vanilla
1 egg, beaten
2½ cups sifted flour
1 teaspoon baking powder

½ teaspoon baking soda
1½ teaspoons salt
½ cup sour cream
1 square (1 oz) semi sweet chocolate, melted
Orange food coloring
Rich Raisin Filling

Cream butter, sugar, orange peel and vanilla until light and fluffy. Beat in egg. Resift flour with baking powder, baking soda and salt. Add to creamed mixture alternately with sour cream. Divide dough in half; blend chocolate into one-half of the dough; tint remaining half with orange food coloring. Cover and chill dough several hours. Prepare and cool Rich Raisin Filling. Roll small amounts of dough at a time (keeping remainder of dough chilled) about 3/8 inches thick. Cut into rounds about 2¾ inches. Spoon 1½ teaspoons filling onto center of half the rounds; top with remaining round with cutout faces (make a cardboard stencil for a cutting guide.) Press edges of cookies together with floured tines of fork. Place on lightly greased baking sheets. Bake in a hot oven (425 degrees) 8 – 10 minutes or until lightly browned. Cool cookies thoroughly on wire racks before storing. Makes two and one half dozen filled cookies.

Rich Raisin Filling

2 cups dark or golden raisins
2/3 cup orange juice
1/3 cup water
1 cup brown sugar (packed)

2 tablespoons lemon juice
2 tablespoon butter
1 tablespoon cornstarch

Stir all ingredients together. Cook over moderate heat, stirring occasionally, until mixture boils and thickens. Remove from heat and cool. Makes about 1¾ cups filling.

* * * * *

HOLIDAY FRUIT COOKIES

From Mrs. Emil Knaack

1 cup shortening
1 cup brown sugar
1 well-beaten egg
1¾ cup flour
½ teaspoon salt

½ teaspoon soda
¼ cup thick sour milk
¾ cup broken pecans
¾ cup candied cherries
¾ cup dates

Cream shortening and sugar. Sift dry ingredients and add alternately with sour milk to the creamed shortening and sugar. Add fruit and nuts with last addition of flour. Raisins, filberts, pineapple or citron may be added if desired. Drop by teaspoons on greased cookie sheet and put pecan on each. Bake 15 minutes at 400 degrees. Recipe makes 3 dozen cookies.

These cookies can also be frosted, and they keep well.

* * * * *

HUNGARIAN COOKIE

Press Cookies

1 cup butter
½ cup sugar
1 (8 oz) pkg cream cheese

2 egg yolks
3 cups sifted four
¼ teaspoon salt

Cream butter, then add sugar and cream cheese. Add unbeaten egg yolks – and beat thoroughly. Sift dry ingredients in batter. Mix together. Bake 10 – 12 minutes in a 425 degree oven. May be sprinkled with sugar and cinnamon or you may add a teaspoon of lemon or orange extract to the dough.

* * * * *

ICE BOX COOKIES

1 cup butter
2 cups brown sugar (light is best)
2 eggs, well beaten

Sift 3 times:
3½ cups flour
½ teaspoon salt
1 teaspoon soda

Pinch of cinnamon
Pinch of nutmeg

1 cup nutmeats cut or chopped fine.

Roll in long roll, put in icebox overnight. Slice and bake in a quick oven.

* * * * *

LEMON COCONUT COOKIES

1 cup butter
½ cup sugar
1 egg
½ teaspoon grated lemon rind

2 cups sifted enriched flour
¼ teaspoon salt
1 cup shredded coconut, finely chopped

Cream butter, add sugar and continue creaming until light and fluffy. Add egg and lemon rind. Beat well. Sift together flour and salt. Stir flour mixture into creamed mixture. Blend in coconut. Drop by teaspoonfuls on ungreased baking sheet. Bake in a moderately slow oven (325 degrees) until lightly browned around the edges. About
15 – 20 minutes. Makes about 6 dozen 2-inch cookies.

* * * * *

MOLASSES

1 cup molasses
4 tablespoons sugar
1 egg
1 cup sour cream (real thick)

1 teaspoon soda
1 teaspoon cinnamon
2/3 cup raisins
2 cups flour

* * * * *

★ MOLASSES COOKIES

From Mother

1 cup shortening
1 cup light brown sugar
1 cup molasses
2 eggs
1 teaspoon ginger
1 teaspoon cloves

1 teaspoon mace
2 teaspoons cinnamon
½ teaspoon salt
2 teaspoons soda
¼ cup sour milk
4 cups flour

Mix all. Let chill. Drop with teaspoon on greased pan. Then bake in 350 degree oven 12 minutes.

* * * * *

NANCY'S PEPPERMINT COOKIES

From Nancy Schuman, Johnson County, Indiana

1 cup margarine
1 cup brown sugar
1 egg
2 cups sifted all purpose flour

1 teaspoon baking soda
½ teaspoon salt
2 cups quick cooking oats
½ cup crushed peppermint candy

Glaze:

1½ cup sifted confectioners' sugar
3 tablespoons milk
3 tablespoons crushed peppermint candy

Beat margarine and brown sugar in mixing bowl until light and fluffy. Blend in egg. Set aside. Sift together flour, soda and salt. Add dry ingredients to creamed mixture; mix well. Stir in quick oats and peppermint; mixing well. Roll in 1 inch balls and place 2 inches apart on ungreased cookie sheet. Bake for 10 – 12 minutes. Cool 1 minute; remove from cookie sheet. Cool completely. Combine sugar and milk for glaze; mix well. Drizzle glaze over cooled cookies; sprinkle with crushed peppermint candy

Yield: About 4 dozen.

* * * * *

OATMEAL COOKIES

From Mrs. Meier

Good

½ cup shortening – part butter
1 cup brown sugar
¼ cup white sugar
2 eggs
1½ cup flour
1 teaspoon soda

¾ teaspoon salt
¾ teaspoon cinnamon
1 teaspoon vanilla
2 cups quick cooking rolled oats
¼ cup chopped nuts
½ cup cut-up raisins

Cream shortening, add sugar and mix well. Add eggs and cream well. Sift flour before measuring. Add all dry ingredients to flour and sift into creamed mixture. Add rolled oats, nuts and raisins; mix well.

Bake at 350 degrees for about 10 minutes. Let cool a minute before removing from cookie sheet. Cool on a wire rack. This is a mild oatmeal cookie enjoyed by young and old.

* * * * *

ORANGE COOKIES

1½ cups sugar
½ cup lard
½ cup butter
1 cup sour milk
1 teaspoon soda
½ teaspoon salt

1 teaspoon baking powder
3 eggs
4 cups flour
2 oranges, grated
2 tablespoons orange juice

* * * * *

ORANGE COOKIES

From Mrs. Marjorie Smith Lee

1 cup butter
1½ cups white sugar
3 eggs
1 cup sour milk
Rind and juice of 1 orange

1 teaspoon baking powder
1 teaspoon soda
½ teaspoon salt
3 2/3 cups flour

In a large mixing bowl cream butter and sugar. Add egg, sour milk, orange rind and juice and mix. Add dry ingredients and mix well. Drop by teaspoons on greased cookie sheet. Bake 10 – 12 minutes at 350 degrees. Makes about 6 dozen.

Frosting

4 cups powdered sugar
5 tablespoons butter
4 – 5 tablespoons milk
1 teaspoon vanilla

Frost each cookie when cooled.

* * * * *

PEANUT BUTTER & JELLY CRUNCHIES

½ cup shortening
½ cup peanut butter
½ cup brown sugar, packed
½ cup granulated sugar
½ teaspoon vanilla

1 egg
1½ cup sifted flour
1 teaspoon soda
1 teaspoon salt
Red and Green jelly

Combine shortening and peanut butter. Add sugars and vanilla and mix until fluffy. Add egg and beat well. Sift together flour, soda, and salt and blend into sugar mixture. Shape into balls 1 inch in diameter. Place on cookie sheet 3 inches apart. With thumb, press deep hole in center of each cookie. If the sides start to crack pinch together with fingers. Bake in a moderate oven (375 degrees) about 10 minutes or until slightly browned.

Remove cookies from cookie sheet while warm and place on a cooling rack. Put ½ teaspoon red or green jelly in the center of each cookie. Makes 2½ dozen.

* * * * *

PECAN FROSTED POPPYSEED COOKIES

¾ cup butter
1 1/3 cups sugar
¼ cup light molasses

1 egg
1 cup pumpkin
1 teaspoon vanilla

Sift together:
2½ cups flour
1 teaspoon baking powder

1 teaspoon baking soda
¾ teaspoon salt

1/3 cup poppy seeds
1 cup chopped pecans

Mix in order given. Drop by rounded teaspoonfuls on greased cookie sheets. Bake at 350 degrees for 10 – 12 minutes. Frost when cool.

Frosting

¼ cup butter
2 cups powdered sugar
1 teaspoon cinnamon

1 tablespoon light molasses
¼ cup chopped pecans

Beat together and add 1 tablespoon of cream until of spreading consistency. Place a pecan half on top if desired.

* * * * *

PECAN SNAPPERS

2 eggs
2/3 cup shortening
1 package Betty Crocker German chocolate cake mix
Pecan halves
Browned Butter Icing

Heat oven to 375 degrees. Beat eggs, shortening and about half of the cake mix (dry) until smooth. Stir in remaining cake mix. For each cookie, place 3 pecan halves with ends touching in center on ungreased backing sheet. Shape dough into 1 inch balls. Place 1 ball in center of each group of nuts. Bake 8 – 10 minutes. Cool slightly before removing from baking sheet. Cool and frost. About 4 ½ dozen cookies.

Browned Butter Icing

1/3 cup butter or margarine
3 cups confectioners' sugar
1 ½ teaspoons vanilla
about 2 tablespoons milk

Heat butter in saucepan over medium heat until a delicate brown. Stir in sugar, vanilla and milk. Beat until frosting is smooth and is spreading consistency.

* * * * *

PINEAPPLE COOKIES

½ cup shortening
½ cup brown sugar
½ cup white sugar
½ cup drained crushed pineapple
½ cup nut meats
1 egg, well beaten

¼ teaspoon salt
¼ teaspoon soda
1 teaspoon baking powder
2 cups flour
1 teaspoon vanilla

Cream shortening with sugars, add egg, pineapple and flavoring. Beat thoroughly. Sift flour, measure and sift with soda, baking powder and salt. Add nuts to flour mixture. Add dry ingredients to creamed shortening. Mix thoroughly. Drop by teaspoonful onto well oiled baking sheet. Bake in hot oven (425 degrees) for 10 minutes.

* * * * *

POWDERED SUGAR DROPS

Mrs. Arleigh Frautschy, Winning Recipe

1 cup powdered sugar
1 cup butter
1 egg
Cream the mixture well and add 1 teaspoon vanilla and cream again.
Sift together:
3 cups sifted cake flour
¼ teaspoon salt
½ teaspoon soda
½ teaspoon cream of tarter
Blend mixtures together.
Roll the mixture into small balls and press down on cookie sheet with the bottom of a glass dipped in granulated sugar.
Bake for 15 minutes in 350 degree oven.

* * * * *

PRUNE CIRCLE COOKIES

1 cup uncooked Sunsweet prunes
1/3 cup water
1/3 cup granulated sugar
1 teaspoon lemon juice
2/3 cup shortening (Crisco)
1¼ cups brown sugar, packed

2 large eggs
1 teaspoon vanilla
2 cups sifted all purpose flour
1 teaspoon salt
½ teaspoon baking powder
½ teaspoon soda

Snip prunes into small pieces. Add water. Cook stirring often for 5 minutes or until water is absorbed. Stir in granulated sugar and lemon juice; cool.

Cream shortening, brown sugar, eggs and vanilla together well. (Mixture will look slightly curdled).

Resift flour with salt, baking powder and soda. Blend into creamed mixture. Drop by level tablespoons onto lightly greased baking sheets with room for spreading. Top each with a level teaspoonful of prune mixture. Top filling with ½ teaspoon additional cookie dough, spreading it slightly to partially cover filling.

Bake at 375 degrees for 10 – 12 minutes until edges are lightly browned.

Let stand a minute then remove with a broad spatula to wire racks to cool. Makes about 40 cookies.

* * * * *

RHUBARB BAR COOKIE

Cook together and cool:
1½ cup finely cut rhubarb
1 cup raisins
¼ cup water

½ cup butter or
shortening
1½ cups sugar

2 eggs
½ teaspoon salt
2½ cups flour
1 teaspoon baking soda
1 cup chopped nuts.

Cream together: Add

Bake in large baking sheet, greased and floured at 350 degrees for 25 minutes. Cool, and then frost with powdered sugar frosting.

★ ★ ★ ★ ★

ROCK'S

2 cups brown sugar
1 cup lard or butter
2 cups flour
2 cups oatmeal (fine)
1 cup seeded raisins
½ cup walnuts, or other nuts

½ teaspoon salt
1 teaspoon soda (Dissolved in 2 teaspoons boiling water)
2 teaspoons cinnamon
½ teaspoon cloves
2 eggs

Mix well. Drop with spoon. Bake in a quick oven.

★ ★ ★ ★ ★

★ SNICKERDOODLE COOKIES

1 cup butter
¾ cup firmly packed brown sugar
¾ cup granulated sugar
2 eggs, well-beaten
2 cups sifted flour
½ teaspoon salt

1 teaspoon soda
1 teaspoon cinnamon
1½ cups quick or old fashioned oats, uncooked
Cinnamon-sugar

In large mixer bowl beat butter until creamy. Add sugars, mix until light and fluffy. Add eggs; mix well. Sift together flour, salt, soda and cinnamon. Add sifted dry ingredients to creamed mixture; mix until well combined. Stir in oats. Form dough into 1-inch balls. Roll in cinnamon-sugar.

Place on greased cookie sheets 1-inch apart. Bake in preheated hot oven (400 degrees) 8 – 10 minutes. Remove cookies from cookie sheets. Cool completely on wire rack. Store in tightly covered container.

Yield: Four and one-half to five dozen.

★ ★ ★ ★ ★

SNOW DROPS

2¼ cups sifted flour
¼ teaspoon salt
1 cup butter
½ cup sifted confectioners' sugar

1 teaspoon vanilla
¾ cup chopped walnuts
¼ cup confectioners' sugar

Combine and sift flour and salt. Cream butter. Add the ½ cup sugar and vanilla and blend. Add dry ingredients and nuts. Mix thoroughly. Chill dough. Form into balls 1 inch in diameter. Place 1 inch apart on unbuttered cooking sheet. Bake in a hot oven (400 degrees) for 10 – 12 minutes. While warm, roll in remaining ¼ cup sugar. Cool. Roll in sugar again. Makes 4 dozen cookies.

* * * * *

SPECIAL K COOKIES – NO-BAKE

From Jean

Bring to a boil:
½ cup Karo Syrup
½ cup sugar

Remove from heat and add
¾ cup peanut butter

Stir until smooth, and then pour over
4 cups Special K

Stir until evenly coated, press in buttered pan and frost.

Frosting

Melt in double boiler
1 (6 oz) pkg butterscotch chips
1 (6 oz) pkg chocolate chips

* * * * *

SPECIAL K FRUIT COOKIES

2 cups sifted flour * [add more flour]
1 teaspoon baking powder
1 teaspoon baking soda
½ teaspoon salt
1 cup soft butter or margarine * [half Crisco]
2 cups brown sugar, firmly packed

2 eggs
1 teaspoon vanilla flavoring
1 cup flaked coconut
1 cup broken walnut meats
½ cup raisins
4 cups Kellogg's Special K

1. Sift together flour, baking powder, soda and salt.
2. Blend butter and sugar until light and fluffy. Add eggs and vanilla; beat well.
3. Add sifted dry ingredients, coconut, walnut meats and raisins; mix well. Stir in Special K. Drop by tablespoonfuls onto greased baking sheets.
4. Bake in moderate oven (375 degrees) for about 10 minutes or until lightly browned.

Yield: about 5 dozen cookies, 2½ inches in diameter.
* denotes notes added to the recipe

* * * * *

SPICE DATE COOKIES

Buttered cookie sheets. Yield: 6 dozen. Preheated 400 degree oven.

½ cup (1 stick) butter, softened
1½ cups firmly packed brown sugar
1 teaspoon vanilla
2 eggs, well beaten
2½ cups flour
1 teaspoon soda

½ teaspoon baking powder
½ teaspoon salt
½ teaspoon cinnamon
¼ teaspoon nutmeg
1 cup dairy sour cream
2 cups chopped pitted dates

Thoroughly cream together butter, sugar and vanilla. Add eggs; mix well. Sift dry ingredients together. Add to creamed mixture alternately with sour cream. Stir in dates. Drop from teaspoon about two inches apart on cookie sheet. Optional – top each cookie with a walnut half. Bake about 10 minutes or until browned.

* * * * *

SUGAR COOKIES

¾ cup sifted flour
½ teaspoon baking powder
¼ teaspoon salt
3 tablespoons fat
2 tablespoons brown sugar

2 tablespoons white sugar
½ egg
½ teaspoon vanilla
1 teaspoon milk
flour for rolling

Sift flour once, measure then add baking powder, salt, mix well and sift again. Cream fat, beat in sugar gradually, and add egg, vanilla and milk. Stir in flour gradually; remove dough to a slightly floured board. With a well floured rolling pin, roll dough 1/8" thick, cut with cookie cutter. Place on ungreased baking sheet. Bake at 400 degrees for 8-10 minutes.

* * * * *

★ SUGAR COOKIES

375 degree oven

Cream:
1½ cups confectioner's sugar
1 cup butter or margarine

Mix in:
1 egg
1 teaspoon vanilla
½ teaspoon almond extract

Sift together and add:
2½ cups all-purpose flour
1 teaspoon soda
1 teaspoon cream or tartar

Refrigerate 2 – 3 hours. Heat oven. Roll only half of the dough at one time. Bake about 7 minutes.

* * * * *

SWEET CHOCOLATE CHIP COOKIES

2½ cups unsifted flour
1 teaspoon baking soda
1 teaspoon salt
1 cup butter, softened
¾ cup sugar
¾ cup packed brown sugar

1 teaspoon vanilla extract
2 eggs
1 (12 oz) pkg Nestle Sweet Chocolate morsels
1 cup chopped nuts

Preheat oven to 375 degrees. In small bowl combine flour, baking soda and salt. Set aside. In large bowl combine butter, sugar and brown sugar and vanilla extract. Beat until creamy. Beat in eggs. Gradually add flour mixture, mixing well. Stir in chocolate morsels and nuts. Drop by rounded measuring spoonfuls on ungreased cookie sheets. Bake at 375 degrees for 8 – 10 minutes.

* * * * *

SWISS COOKIES

From Lillian Gempler (passed down from her grandmother)

MAILAENDERLI

1½ pounds flour (4 cups = 1 pound)
2 cups sugar
¾ cup butter
3 eggs, add one at a time

1 teaspoon cinnamon
2 teaspoons baking powder
grated rind of one lemon
1 tablespoon lemon juice

Mix in the usual manner. Roll out and cut with cookie cutter. Brush top of cookies with beaten egg before baking in slow oven.

* * * * *

THREE PART COOKIES

Good
Plain cookies

(First part)
4½ cups cake flour
1 cup shortening
Cut the shortening into the flour as for pie crust and add ½ teaspoon salt.

(Second part)
2 eggs, beaten
1 cup sugar
Beat the sugar into the eggs.

(Third part)
4 tablespoons sweet milk
1 teaspoon vanilla
1 teaspoon soda
nutmeg, if desired.

Add the eggs and sugar mixture to part-1, and then add mixture from part-3 to part-1. It will not be necessary to add any more flour for rolling. The cookies may be rolled and baked immediately. Cut with animal cookie cutters. Bake 14 minutes at 425 degrees. Make 53 large cookies.

If you want to keep them soft, put them in a covered receptacle.
(Christmas cookie)

 * * * * *

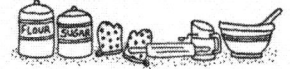  

TOLL HOUSE COOKIES

1 cup shortening or butter
¾ cup honey
¾ cup maple syrup

Add
2 eggs, well beaten

Sift together:
2½ cups flour
1 teaspoon soda
½ teaspoon salt

Then add:
½ cup nutmeats, chopped
2 (7 oz) pkgs semi-sweet chocolate chips

Last add 1 teaspoon vanilla. Drop by teaspoonfuls.

Makes 100 cookies.

* * * * *

TRICIA'S CHOCOALTE CHIP COOKIES

½ cup butter
6 tablespoons brown sugar
6 tablespoons white sugar
½ teaspoon vanilla
1 egg

½ teaspoon soda
½ teaspoon salt
1 cup plus 2 tablespoons sifted flour
½ cup chopped nuts
½ cup chocolate pieces

Cream butter. Slowly add sugars and beat until creamy. Then beat in vanilla and egg. Sift together and stir into mixture the soda, salt, and flour. Then stir in nuts and chocolate pieces. Drop batter from a teaspoon onto a greased cookie sheet and bake 8 minutes in 375 degree oven. Keep blobs of dough wide apart on pan. Makes about 2 dozen.

* * * * *

TOFFEE CRUNCH COOKIES

1½ cup sifted flour
½ teaspoon baking soda
½ teaspoon salt
½ cup butter
¾ cup (packed) brown sugar

1 egg
1 teaspoon vanilla
1 cup finely chopped English toffee candy bars
1/3 cup coarsely chopped pecans

Combine and sift flour, soda and salt. Cream butter. Add sugar, egg and vanilla; mix until smooth and creamy. Stir in dry ingredients; blend in chopped candy bars and pecans.

Drop tablespoonfuls 2 inches apart on greased baking sheets. Bake in moderate (350 degree) oven until done. 12 – 15 minutes. Remove from baking sheets; cool. Yield: About three dozen cookies.

* * * * *

UNBAKED CHOCOLATE COOKIES

Yield: 2 – 3 dozen

2 cups sugar
½ cup (1 stick) butter
1 square chocolate
½ cup milk

3 cups quick cooking oatmeal
¼ cup peanut butter
1 teaspoon vanilla

Place first four ingredients in large saucepan. Bring mixture to a full rolling boil. Remove from heat and add remaining ingredients. Mix well. Drop from spoon onto waxed paper. Allow to cool. In hot weather, store cookies in the refrigerator.

* * * * *

WHEATENE PEANUT BUTTER COOKIES

2¼ cups sifted unbleached flour
½ teaspoon soda
1 teaspoon baking powder
½ cup butter or margarine
½ cup shortening
1 cup sugar

1 cup brown sugar, firmly packed
¼ cup Wheatena, uncooked
2 eggs, lightly beaten
1 cup crunchy peanut butter
2 teaspoons vanilla

Sift together flour, soda and baking powder. Cream shortenings with sugars and Wheatena. Add eggs, peanut butter and vanilla; mix well. Stir in sifted dry ingredients and mix thoroughly. Roll dough into balls about the size of a walnut and place on ungreased cookie sheet, about ½ inches apart. Press with tines of fork to make crisscross. Bake in pre-heated 375 degree oven 10 – 12 minutes, or until test done. Makes about 6½ dozen cookies.

* * * * *

WHITE DROP COOKIES

From Mr. Hjalmar Duffy

Good

½ cup butter
½ cup shortening
1 cup white sugar
1 cup confectioners' sugar
2 eggs
1 teaspoon salt

1 cup cooking oil
1 teaspoon vanilla
4 cups plus 4 tablespoons flour
1 teaspoon soda
1 teaspoon cream of tartar

Mix ingredients well and form into balls. Roll in sugar and flatten with glass or fork. Bake at 350 degrees for 12 – 15 minutes. Yield: About 5 dozen

★ ★ ★ ★ ★

Dessert Bars

APRICOT BARS

1 cup dried apricots
2/3 cup water
1 cup all-purpose flour
6 tablespoons (¾ stick) butter or margarine
1½ cups brown sugar, firmly packed

1 tablespoon cornstarch
¼ teaspoon salt
2 teaspoons grated orange peel
2 tablespoons orange juice
2 eggs, beaten
1½ cup flaked coconut

Cut apricots in small pieces, combine with water, cover and simmer for 20 minutes. Meanwhile, mix flour, butter and ½ cup sugar. Press crumbly mixture into greased 11 x 7 (or 9 x 9) pan. Bake at 350 degrees for 20 minutes. Mix 1 cup sugar, cornstarch and salt. Stir into undrained apricots and cook until thickened, stirring constantly. Remove from heat. Stir in remaining ingredients, reserving a little coconut. Spread apricot mixture over baked crust. Sprinkle top with reserved coconut. Bake at 350 degrees for 25 minutes. Cool in pan. Cut into bars. Makes 27 – 30 bars.

* * * * *

BROWNIES

From Marie Blum

1 cup sugar
¼ cup butter
2 eggs

2 squares chocolate
¾ cup flour
1 tablespoon vanilla
nuts

Bake at 250 – 300 degrees.

* * * * *

BROWN SUGAR CHEWS

1½ cup sifted flour
2 teaspoons baking powder
1 teaspoon salt
½ cup shortening
1¼ cup firmly packed dark brown sugar

½ cup flaked coconut
¾ cups chopped pecans
2 eggs
¼ cup milk
1 teaspoon vanilla

Sift together the flour, baking powder and salt. Cut or rub in shortening until mixture is crumbly. Mix in brown sugar, coconut and pecans. Beat eggs until thick and ivory-colored; add milk and vanilla and beat enough to combine. Add to flour mixture. Mix well. Turn into greased baking pan (9 x 13) and spread evenly. Bake in moderate oven (350 degrees) 40 – 45 minutes. Cool in pan placed on wire rack about 10 minutes. Cut into bars. Cool bars entirely before removing from pan with spatula. Store in tightly covered container.

* * * * *

BUTTER MILK BARS

From Madison Paper

1¼ cups sugar
¾ cup brown sugar
2 cups flour
½ cup butter
½ cup chopped nuts

1 egg
1 cup buttermilk
1 teaspoon soda
¾ teaspoon salt
¾ teaspoon cinnamon

Mix sugars and flour, cut in butter as for pie crust. Combine two cups of this mixture with the nutmeats; press in bottom of 9 x 13 pan.

Combine remaining ingredients; heat until smooth. Add remaining crumb mixture. Beat again hard. Spread over unbaked layer in pan. Bake 45 minutes at 350 degrees. When completely cool, sprinkle with confectioners' sugar or frost. Cut into bars.

* * * * *

BUTTERSCOTCH BARS

½ cup butter or margarine
2 cups packed brown sugar
2 eggs
1 teaspoon vanilla
2 cups sifted all purpose flour

2 teaspoons baking powder
¼ teaspoon salt
1 cup flaked coconut
1 cup chopped peanuts

In 2 quart saucepan, melt butter or margarine. Remove from heat. Stir in brown sugar. Add eggs, one at a time, beating well after each addition. Add vanilla. Sift together flour, baking powder and salt. Add flour mixture, coconut, and peanuts to ingredients in saucepan. Mix thoroughly. Spread in greased 15 x 10 inch baking pan. Bake in 350 degree oven for 25 minutes. Cut into bars while warm. Dust with powdered sugar. Remove from pan when almost cool. Makes 3 dozen.

* * * * *

CARAMEL CHOCO-SQUARES

Good

About 50 (14-oz) pkg light caramels
1/3 cup evaporated milk
1 package (17 ½ oz) German chocolate cake mix
¾ cup butter, melted
1/3 cup evaporated milk
1 cup chopped nuts
1 cup (6 oz) pkg semi-sweet chocolate pieces

In top of double boiler, combine caramels and 1/3 cup evaporated milk. Cook over hot water, stirring constantly until caramels are melted. Set aside.

Generously grease and lightly flour a 9 x 13 baking pan. In large bowl combine dry cake mix, butter 1/3 cup evaporated milk and nuts. By hand stir until dough holds together.

Press half of dough into prepared pan; reserve remaining dough for topping. Bake in moderate (350 degree) oven for 6 minutes. Sprinkle chocolate pieces over baked crust. Spread caramel mixture over chocolate pieces. Crumble reserved dough over caramel mixture.

Return to oven and bake for 15 – 18 minutes. Cool slightly, refrigerate about 30 minutes to set caramel layer. Cut into bars. Yield: 36 bars.

* * * * *

CHERRY PINEAPPLE BARS

From Better Homes & Garden

2 cups sifted all purpose flour
1 cup brown sugar
½ teaspoon salt
1 cup butter or margarine
½ cup granulated sugar

2 tablespoons cornstarch
1 (8 ¾ oz.) crushed pineapple
2 beaten egg yolks
1 cup maraschino cherries chopped

In small bowl, combine flour, brown sugar and salt. Cut in butter or margarine till crumbly. Set aside 1 cup crumb mixture. Press remaining crumb mixture on bottom of 9 x 13 baking pan. Bake in 350 degree oven for 15 minutes. Cool slightly while preparing topping.

In sauce pan, combine sugar and cornstarch. Stir in undrained pineapple and the egg yolks. Cook over medium heat stirring constantly till mixture thickens and bubbles. Remove from heat. Stir in cherries. Spread evenly over baked layer. Sprinkle on reserved crumb mixture. Bake in 350 degree oven for 30 minutes more. Cool before cutting into bars. Makes 2½ dozen bars.

* * * * *

CHEWY CARAMEL BROWNIES

From Good Housekeeping

2 cups packed light brown sugar
1 cup all-purpose flour
1 cup chopped nuts
½ cup shortening

2 eggs
2 teaspoons baking powder
2 teaspoons vanilla
¾ teaspoon salt

Preheat oven 350 degrees.

Grease and flour 15 ½ x 10 ½ jelly roll pan.

Into large bowl, measure all ingredients. With mixer at medium speed, beat all ingredients until well mixed, occasionally scraping bowl with spatula. Evenly spread in pan. Bake 25 minutes or until golden brown. Cool brownies in pan 5 minutes. Cut and with a pancake turner remove to wire rack to cool.

* * * * *

CHOCOLATE CHERRY BARS

1 pkg Pillsbury fudge cake mix
1 (21-oz) can cherry fruit filling
1 teaspoon almond extract
2 eggs, beaten

Frosting

1 cup sugar
5 tablespoons butter or margarine
1/3 cup milk
1 (6-oz) pkg (1 cup) semi-sweet chocolate pieces

Preheat oven to 350 degrees. Using solid shortening or margarine (not oil), grease and flour a 15 x 10 inch jelly roll pan. In large bowl, combine the first four ingredients. By hand, stir until well mixed. Pour into prepared pan.

Bake jelly roll pan 20 – 30 minutes or until toothpick inserted in center comes out clean.

In small saucepan, combine sugar, butter and milk. Boil, stirring constantly, one minute.
Remove from heat; stir in chocolate pieces until smooth. Pour over bars.
Yield: about three dozen bars.

* * * * *

CHOCOLATE CREAM CHEESE BROWNIES

1 (4-oz) package German sweet chocolate
2 tablespoons butter or margarine
2 eggs
1 teaspoon vanilla
¾ cup sugar
½ cup sifted all purpose flour
½ teaspoon baking powder

¼ teaspoon salt
½ cup chopped walnuts
1 (3-oz) pkg cream cheese, softened
¼ cup sugar
1 egg
½ teaspoon vanilla

In saucepan, melt chocolate and butter or margarine. Cool. In small bowl, beat together the 2 eggs and 1 teaspoon vanilla, gradually add the ¾ cup sugar. Continue beating till thick and lemon colored. Sift together flour, baking powder and salt. Add to egg mixture, beating well. Blend in cooled chocolate mixture and the nuts. Set aside. In mixer bowl, cream together cream cheese and the remaining sugar till fluffy. Blend in the remaining egg and vanilla. Spread half of the chocolate mixture in greased and floured 8 x 8 x 2 baking pan. Pour cheese mixture over top with spoonfuls of the chocolate mixture. Using a narrow spatula, swirl through layers to marble. Bake in 350 degree oven for 40 – 45 minutes. Cut in squares when cool. Makes 16.

* * * * *

★ CHOCOLATE REFRESHERS

Note: Very Good
(Prize winner in 11th Pillsbury Bake off)

1 ½ cup sifted all purpose flour
¾ teaspoon soda
½ teaspoon salt
1 ½ cups dates, cut in pieces
¾ cup firmly packed brown sugar
½ cup water

½ cup butter
1 cup (6 oz) pkg semi-sweet morsels
2 unbeaten eggs
½ cup orange juice
½ cup milk
1 cup chopped walnuts

Sift flour with soda and salt. Combine dates, brown sugar, water, butter in large saucepan. Cook over low heat, stirring constantly until dates soften. Remove from heat. Stir in chocolate morsels. Beat in eggs. Add dry ingredients alternately with orange juice and milk. Blend thoroughly after each addition. Stir in walnuts. Bake in well greased 15 x 10 jelly roll pan at 350 degrees for 25 – 30 minutes. Cool. Spread with orange glaze. Cut in bars.

Orange Glaze

1 ½ cup sifted confectioner's sugar
2 tablespoons butter

1 – 2 tablespoons grated orange rind
2 – 3 tablespoons cream

Combine sugar, butter and orange rind. Blend in cream until of spreading consistency.

* * * * *

★ COCONUT CHEWS

From Jean

½ cup brown sugar, firmly packed
½ cup shortening (half butter)
1 cup sifted all purpose flour

2 eggs well beaten
½ cup brown sugar, firmly packed
½ cup Karo syrup (light or dark)
1 teaspoon vanilla

1 teaspoon baking powder
2 tablespoons flour
½ teaspoon salt
1 cup shredded coconut (southern style)
1 cup coarsely chopped walnuts

Blend sugar and shortening. Stir in flour. Pat out mixture into bottom of ungreased pan 9 x 9 x 2. Bake in a moderate (350 degree) oven for 10 minutes. Meanwhile blend eggs and brown sugar. Stir in Karo syrup and vanilla. Add flour, baking powder and salt. Mix well. Stir in coconut and nuts, and spread over bottom layer. Return to oven and bake 25 minutes longer or until top is golden brown. Cool in pan, cut into finger length bars. Makes 24 bars.

* * * * *

COCONUT PECAN BARS

2 cups sifted flour
1 teaspoon baking powder
1 teaspoon salt
1 cup butter
2 cups firmly packed brown sugar

2 eggs
2 teaspoons vanilla
1 can (3 ½ oz) flaked coconut
1 cup chopped pecans

Sift together flour, baking powder, and salt. Cream butter well. Add brown sugar, eggs and vanilla. Beat until smooth and creamy. Add sifted dry ingredients. Mix well. Stir in coconut and pecans. Spread in buttered 10 x 15 inch jelly roll pan. Bake in a moderate oven (350 degrees) about 25 minutes or until done. Cool. Sprinkle with confectioners' sugar and cut into bars.

Make about 3½ dozen 2½ x 1½ inch bars.

Rich but delicious.

* * * * *

DOUBLE-SCOTCH PECAN BARS

From Parade's Test Kitchen

Good

¾ cup softened butter of margarine
1 cup firmly packed dark brown sugar
1 egg
½ teaspoon vanilla
2 cups sifted all-purpose flour
¾ teaspoon salt

½ teaspoon baking powder
¼ cup milk
1 (6-oz) package butterscotch pieces, (1 cup)
1 cup flaked coconut
1 cup chopped pecans

Cream together butter and sugar; stir in egg and vanilla. Mix and sift flour, salt and baking powder. Add alternately to creamed mixture with milk. Fold in butterscotch pieces, coconut and pecans. Spread evenly on greased cookie sheet into a 14 x 10 inch rectangle. Bake in a moderate oven (350 degrees) 15 minutes. Cool. Spread with Butterscotch Topping if desired. Cut in bars 2½ x 1 inch. Makes approximately 60 bars.

Butterscotch Topping

1 (6-oz) pkg butterscotch morsels, (1 cup)
1 teaspoon salad oil
2 tablespoons water

Melt butterscotch morsels with salad oil over hot (not boiling) water. Add the 2 tablespoons water; stir vigorously until smooth.

* * * * *

DATE BARS

3 eggs
1 cup sugar mixed in eggs
1 cup flour
salt

1 teaspoon baking powder
½ cup nuts
dates
2 tablespoons hot water (last)

* * * * *

EASY ALMOND CRUNCH BARS

NOTE: The recipe given below was a $5,000 winner for Mrs. Milton Beckwith, North Franklin, Conn at the Pillsbury Bake-off Feb 24 in California. (No year provided.)

1 package Pillsbury Coconut Almond or Coconut Pecan Frosting Mix
1 cup Pillsbury's Best All Purpose, unbleached or Self-Rising Flour
½ cup butter or margarine, melted
1-2 teaspoons almond extract

Preheat oven to 400 degrees. (Lightly spoon flour into measuring cup; level off.) In large bowl, combine first four (4) ingredients; blend well. Press into ungreased 13 x 9 inch pan. Bake 10 – 12 minutes until golden brown. In small bowl, combine Glaze ingredients, blend until smooth. Drizzle over bars. Cut into bars while still warm. 2 – 3 dozen bars

Glaze:

1 cup powdered sugar

¼ - ½ teaspoon almond extract

2 – 3 tablespoons milk

* * * * *

FRENCH BARS

From Mrs. Julian Johnson, Blanchardville.

NOTE: Good
Fourth and Final Winner in Lafayette County June Dairy Bar Bake-Off.

2 eggs, well beaten
1 cup brown sugar
¾ cup sour cream
¾ teaspoon baking soda
1 cup flour – unsifted

½ teaspoon cinnamon
¼ teaspoon salt
¾ cup chopped nuts
¾ cup cut-up dates
½ cup toasted flaked coconut

Add sugar to eggs and beat till thick. Stir in sour cream. Blend in dry ingredients, and then stir in nuts, dates and coconut. Do not over mix batter. Spread in lightly greased jelly roll pan. Bake in moderate oven (350 degrees) for 20 minutes. Yield: 40 1½ x 2½ bars. Frost with Orange Butter Frosting before cutting.

Orange Butter Frosting

1 cup confectioner's sugar
¼ cup butter
1½ tablespoons orange juice

¼ teaspoon salt
½ teaspoon grated orange rind

Combine ingredients and beat until creamy. Spread on cooled bars.

* * * * *

FROSTED GINGER BARS

1¼ cup sifted flour
½ teaspoon soda
½ teaspoon cinnamon
½ teaspoon ginger
¼ teaspoon cloves
¼ teaspoon salt

½ cup butter
¼ cup water
½ cup molasses
½ cup firmly packed brown sugar
2 eggs, slightly beaten
Frosting

Sift together flour, soda, spices and salt. Heat butter and water together until butter melts. Pour into mixing bowl. Stir in molasses and brown sugar. Beat in eggs. Add sifted dry ingredients. Blend well. Pour into buttered 12 x 9 pan. Bake in a moderate oven (350 degrees) 20 – 25 minutes or until done. Cool to lukewarm and frost with frosting. Cut into bars when cool.

Makes about 2½ dozen, 2½ x 1½ bars.

Frosting

2 tablespoons butter
2 cups sifted confectioners' sugar

2 tablespoons half and half
1 teaspoon grated lemon rind

Cream butter, stir in confectioners' sugar, half and half and lemon rind. Beat until smooth. If nuts are a favorite at your house, add.

* * * * *

GERMAN CHOCOLATE BAR COOKIES

½ cup butter or margarine
1 package German chocolate cake mix
3 cups miniature marshmallows
1 (6 oz) pkg butterscotch pieces

1½ cup flaked coconut
1 cup chopped pecans
1 (14 oz) can sweetened condensed milk

Heat oven to 350 degrees. In oven, melt butter in jelly roll pan. Rotate pan until butter covers bottom. Sprinkle cake mix (dry) in pan. Sprinkle marshmallows, butterscotch pieces, coconut and nuts over cake mix in order listed. Pour milk evenly over top. Bake about 25 minutes or until golden brown. Run knife around edges to loosen sides. Cool. Cut into bars 3 x 1½ inches. 30 bars.

* * * * *

GRAHAM CRACKER BARS

Lay graham crackers on bottom of 14 x 10 pan.

Cook filling:
½ cup (1 stick) butter
½ cup milk
1 cup sugar
1 egg, beaten

Add
1 cup coconut
1 cup crushed graham crackers
nuts

Cook until thicken.
Take off stove and cool slightly.

Spread this mixture on top of graham crackers. Put another layer of graham crackers on top of mixture and frost with powdered sugar flavored with orange juice.

* * * * *

HONEY MOON SQUARES

From Mr. Kenneth Waelti

1 cup brown sugar
1½ cup flour
pinch salt
1½ cup oatmeal
vanilla
½ teaspoon soda (sifted with flour)
1 cup butter or other shortening

Filling:
1½ cups pitted dates, raisins, or pineapple
½ cup sugar
1 cup water
Boil together until thick. Mix the first ingredients. Line a greased pan with ½ of mixture. Put in cooled filling and add balance of mixture. Bake in moderate oven for 20-30 minutes.

* * * * *

LAYERED FUDGE BARS

From Dorothy Leopold

2 cups flour
1 teaspoon baking powder
½ teaspoon soda
1 teaspoon salt
½ cup butter

2 cups sugar
2 eggs
1 1/3 cups milk
4 oz unsweetened chocolate, melted
1 teaspoon vanilla

Sift together flour, baking powder, soda and salt. Add butter, sugar and 1 cup milk and beat 1½ minute. Add remaining milk, eggs, chocolate and vanilla and beat 1½ minutes longer. Spread ½ of batter in greased 9 x 13 pan, spread cheese filling over batter, and cover with remaining batter. Bake in 350 degree oven for 55 minutes. Cool, cover with chocolate topping.

Cheese Filling

1 (8 oz) pkg cream cheese
2 tablespoons butter
¼ cup sugar
1 tablespoon cornstarch

1 egg
2 tablespoons milk
½ teaspoon vanilla

Mix together and beat until smooth.

Chocolate Topping

¼ cup milk
¼ cup butter
1 oz chocolate, melted

2½ cups powdered sugar
About 1 tablespoon milk

Combine milk and butter. Bring to boil, remove from heat and add chocolate and powdered sugar. Beat; add enough milk to give desired consistency to spread.

* * * * *

LEMON CREAM CHEESERS

From Mrs Gene Aebley

½ cup butter
1 ¼ cup flour
½ cup quick cooking rolled oats
½ cup packed brown sugar
¼ teaspoon salt
1 (8 oz) pkg soft cream cheese

1/3 cup sugar
1 egg
2 teaspoons grated lemon rind
1 tablespoon lemon juice
¼ cup milk

Combine first five ingredients; mix until crumbly. Press half of mixture into bottom of ungreased 8 or 9 inch pan.

Combine remaining ingredients; beat until smooth and creamy. Pour over crust. Top with remaining crumb mixture.

Bake at 350 degrees for 30 – 35 minutes.

Cool, cut into bars. Store in refrigerator. NOTE: A drop or 2 of yellow food coloring may be added to cream cheese mixture if desired for a more colorful appearance.

* * * * *

LEMON RAISIN COCONUT SQUARES

Crust Ingredients:

4 tablespoons butter
1/3 cup firmly packed light brown sugar
1 cup all purpose flour
¼ cup flaked coconut

Topping Ingredients:

2 large eggs
1 cup firmly packed light brown sugar
1 tablespoon grated lemon rind
¼ cup lemon juice

¼ teaspoon salt
1½ cups raisins
¾ cup flaked coconut

Prepare Crust: Line the bottom of a 9 inch square baking pan with a sheet of foil long enough to cover 2 opposite sides of the pan and extend slightly beyond them. Butter foil. In a medium bowl cream butter and sugar. Gradually blend in flour. Work in coconut. Press over bottom of the prepared pan. Bake in a preheated 350 degree oven until edges brown lightly – about 12 minutes. Set aside at room temperature. Leave oven control at 350 degrees.

Prepare Topping: In a medium bowl beat eggs until foamy. Stir in sugar, lemon rind, lemon juice, salt, raisins and coconut. Spread over crust. Return to the 350 degree oven and bake until top is lightly browned, 20 – 25 minutes. Place on a wire rack. Cool. With a sharp knife loosen edges. Grasp foil and lift out of pan. On a cutting board using a sharp heavy knife, cut into squares.

* * * * *

MAGIC COOKIE BARS

1½ cups Kellogg corn flake crumbs
3 tablespoons sugar
½ cup (1 stick) butter or margarine, melted
1 cup coarsely chopped walnuts
1 cup (6 oz) pkg semi-sweet chocolate morsels
1 1/3 cup (3 ½ oz) can flaked coconut
1 can sweetened condense milk

Measure cornflake crumbs, sugar and margarine into 13 x 9 baking pan. Mix thoroughly with back of spoon. Press mixture evenly and firmly in bottom of pan to form crust.
Sprinkle walnuts evenly over crust. Scatter chocolate morsels over walnuts. Sprinkle coconut evenly over chocolate morsels. Pour sweetened condensed milk evenly over coconut.
Bake in moderate oven (350 degrees) about 25 minutes or lightly browned around edges. Cool. Cut into bars.

Yield: 54 magic cookie bars 2 x 1 inch.

* * * * *

PEPPERMINT GINGER BARS

½ cup shortening
½ cup sugar
1 egg, beaten
½ cup light molasses
1½ cup enriched flour
½ teaspoon salt
½ teaspoon baking soda

½ teaspoon ginger
½ teaspoon cinnamon
½ teaspoon ground cloves
½ cup crushed peppermint candy
Peppermint Icing
2 tablespoons crushed peppermint candy

Cream together shortening and sugar until light and fluffy. Blend in egg and molasses. Combine flour, salt, soda and spices; blend into creamed mixture. Stir in ½ cup candy. Spread batter evening in greased 9 x 13 baking pan. Bake in preheated 350 degree oven 25 – 30 minutes or until done. Cool. Frost with Peppermint Icing. Sprinkle remaining candy on top. Cut into Bars.

Make 24 bars.

Peppermint Icing

3½ cups confectioners' sugar
1 (3 oz) pkg cream cheese, softened
2 tablespoons water
½ teaspoon peppermint extract
Red food coloring

Cream together 2 cups confectioners sugar and cream cheese until light and fluffy. Add water, peppermint extract and a few drops food coloring. Blend in remaining sugar.

* * * * *

PINEAPPLE BUTTERSCOTCH BARS

2 cups sifted flour
¾ teaspoon baking powder
¾ teaspoon salt
1/3 cup shortening
2/3 cup dark brown sugar, firmly packed
½ teaspoon vanilla

2 eggs
1 cup drained, canned crushed pineapple
1/3 cup coarsely chopped nuts
1 (8 oz) pkg butterscotch bits
Confectioner's sugar

Sift together flour, baking powder and salt. Cream shortening until light and fluffy, gradually adding the brown sugar. Add vanilla and unbeaten eggs; beat well. Stir in drained pineapple. Add sifted dry ingredients, mixing well. Stir in nuts and butterscotch bits. Spread evenly in a greased 9 x 12 baking pan. Bake in a moderate oven (350 degrees) about 25 minutes, until done. Cool on wire rack for about 15 minutes. Cut into 1 2/3 x 2 inch bars and roll in confectioner's sugar. Makes 36 bars.

* * * * *

PUMPKIN BARS

4 eggs
¾ cup butter
½ teaspoon cinnamon
1 cup nuts (walnuts)
2 cups sugar

2 cups flour
1 teaspoon soda
1 (16 oz) can pumpkin
2 teaspoons baking powder

Mix eggs, sugar, pumpkin and butter. Add remaining ingredients, mix. Pour into greased/floured jelly roll pan. Back 350 degrees 30-35 minutes.

Cream Cheese Frosting
Cream together:
1 (3 oz) pkg cream cheese
6 tablespoons butter
1 teaspoon vanilla

1 teaspoon milk
3 cups powdered sugar

* * * * *

PUMPKIN BARS

From Jean

4 eggs
2 cups sugar
1 (16 oz) can pumpkin
1 cup Crisco (use ½ Crisco and ½ margarine)

2 cups flour
2 teaspoons baking powder
1 teaspoon soda
½ teaspoon cinnamon
¾ cup nuts

Mix eggs, sugar, Crisco/margarine, and pumpkin.
Then add all remaining ingredients.
Put into greased and floured jelly roll pan. (18 x 12).
Bake between 325 and 350 degrees for 30 minutes.

Cream Cheese Frosting

1 (3 oz) pkg cream cheese
6 tablespoons butter (soft)
1 teaspoon vanilla

1 tablespoon milk – (maybe more)
3 cups powdered sugar

* * * * *

PUMPKIN NUT BARS

1 cup flour
1 cup brown sugar, packed
½ cup shortening
2 eggs
¾ cup canned or fresh cooked pumpkin
½ teaspoon salt

1½ teaspoons pumpkin pie spice or
1 teaspoon cinnamon
¼ teaspoon ginger
¼ teaspoon nutmeg
1 teaspoon vanilla
½ cup flake coconut
½ cup chopped nuts

Combine in mixing bowl and beat at medium speed for 2 minutes. Spread in greased 9 x 13 pan. Bake at 350 degrees for 20-25 minutes.

Cool and frost with powdered sugar frosting.

* * * * *

RAGGEDY ANN CEREAL BARS

From Janet Gosse, Sheboygan Falls, WI

First Layer:
Cream together
¼ cup butter
½ cup firmly packed brown sugar

Add
¼ teaspoon salt

Cut creamed mixture into
1 cup sifted all-purpose flour.

Press mixture into greased 9 inch square pan. Bake in moderate oven (350 degrees) for 15 minutes. Top with second layer.

Second Layer:
Beat until fluffy:
2 eggs

Add and beat
1 cup firmly packed brown sugar

Add
¼ teaspoon salt
1 teaspoon vanilla

Stir in:
1 cup ready to eat crisp rice cereal
1 cup chopped English walnuts
1 cup shredded coconut

Spread this mixture over baked layer. Continue baking for 12 minutes. Cool and cut into 2 dozen bars.

* * * * *

SHIRLEYS BARS

9 x 13 pan
Layer as listed:

½ cup or 1 stick butter (melted)
1 cup graham cracker crumbs
1 can angel flake coconut
1 small package chocolate chips
1 small package butterscotch chips
½ cup chopped nuts

Pour over all – 1 can sweetened condensed milk
Bake 30 minutes in 325 degree oven.

* * * * *

SOUR CREAM APPLE SQUARES

2 cups all-purpose or unbleached flour
2 cups firmly packed brown sugar
½ cup butter or margarine, softened
1 cup chopped nuts
1 – 2 teaspoons cinnamon
1 teaspoon soda

½ teaspoon salt
1 cup dairy sour cream
1 teaspoon vanilla
1 egg
2 cups (2 medium) peeled, finely chopped
    apples

Preheat oven to 350 degrees. Lightly spoon flour into measuring cup; level off. In large bowl, combine first three ingredients; blend at low speed until crumbly. Stir in nuts. Press 2¾ cups crumb mixture into ungreased 13 x 9 pan. To remaining mixture, add cinnamon, soda, salt, sour cream, vanilla and egg; blend well. Stir in apples. Spoon evenly over base.

Bake 25 – 35 minutes until toothpick inserted in center comes out clean. Cut into squares; serve with whipped cream, if desired.

Yield: 12 – 15 squares.

* * * * *

TOASTED COCONUT CAKE SQUARE

1 package German chocolate cake mix
1 cup chopped pecans
1 (6 oz) pkg semisweet chocolate pieces (1 cup)
1 cup flaked coconut
Easy Icing

Heat oven to 350 degrees. Prepare cake mix as directed on package except – pour batter into greased and floured jellyroll pan (15½ x 10½ x1). Sprinkle pecans, chocolate pieces and coconut over batter. Bake 25 – 30 minutes. Cool. Drizzle with Easy icing. Serve with ice cream or frozen whipped topping, thawed. About 35, 2-inch squares.

Easy Icing:

Mix
2 cups powdered sugar
2 tablespoons water
Stir in additional water, 1 teaspoon at a time until icing is desired consistency.

* * * * *

138

ZUCCHINI BARS

From Earl's Mom 8/1980

Very good

2 cups flour
2 teaspoons baking powder
1 teaspoon baking soda
¼ teaspoon salt
2 teaspoons cinnamon

2 cups sugar
1 cup chopped walnuts
1 cup oil
4 eggs, well beaten
2 cups ground or grated zucchini

Mix all together and bake in 11 x 13 pan or cookie sheet for 25 – 30 minutes in 350 degree oven.

* * * * *

Pudding/Custard

BREAD PUDDING

From Mrs. Jake Schutz

3 slices bread (cut in thick cubes)
4 eggs
3 tablespoons sugar
2½ cups milk

1 teaspoon vanilla
¼ teaspoon cinnamon
¼ teaspoon nutmeg
1 cup raisins

Bake about 1 ½ hours at 350 degrees.
Set casserole in pan of water while baking.

* * * * *

RAISIN RICE PUDDING

From Gladys Berger

½ cup rice
4 cups milk
3 tablespoons butter
½ teaspoon salt
½ cup sugar

3 eggs, beaten
2 teaspoons vanilla
1 cup raisins
½ teaspoon cinnamon
1/8 teaspoon nutmeg

Cook rice. Add remaining ingredients. Pour into buttered casserole. Bake in a moderate oven (350 degrees) for 1 – 1½ hours.

* * * * *

VANILLA RICE CUSTARD

From Mrs. Hilda Spain Minneapolis, MINN

A delicious dessert festive enough for company, easy enough for a family affair.

3 tablespoons cooked brown rice
1 cup nut milk or soy milk
1 egg, slightly beaten
3 tablespoons honey
1 teaspoon pure vanilla
½ cup raisins

Mix well and sprinkle cinnamon over top. Bake at 325 degrees about one hour or until silver knife comes out clean.

* * * * *

PIES

Pie Crust

Editor's Note: This is the recipe Granny gave me for pie crust.
1 cup flour
½ cup Crisco
¼ heaping teaspoon baking powder

Mix until crumbly. Then add REAL COLD water until it holds together.

Roll out on a floured board.

* * * * *

BANANA MALLOW PIE

From Jean

Note: 22 wafers = 1 cup crumbs

1. Combing 2 cups vanilla wafer crumbs and 1/3 cup margarine, melted. Press into 9 inch pie plate. Bake at 375 degrees for 8 minutes.
2. Prepare 1 (3 1/8 oz) pkg vanilla pie filling using 1¾ cups milk. Cover surface with transparent wrap. Chill. Fold in 1½ cups Kraft's miniature marshmallows, 1 cup whipped cream.
3. Slice 2 bananas into crust. Pour filling over bananas. Chill several hours or overnight. Serve and make your family go 'bananas'.

* * * * *

CREAM PIE

Filling

2 cups milk scalded
¼ cup sugar
2 tablespoons cornstarch

¼ teaspoon salt
3 egg yolks
1 teaspoon vanilla

Scald milk in top of double boiler. Blend sugar, cornstarch and salt. Stir into scalded milk slowly. Cook over hot water until mixture thickens, stirring constantly. Cover and cook 10 minutes longer. Beat egg yolks. Blend a little hot mixture into beaten yolks. Return to remaining hot mixture in double boiler. Cook 2 minutes, stirring constantly. Cool. Add vanilla. Pour into Sugar Honey Graham Cracker Crumb Crust and top with Meringue.

Meringue

Few grains salt
3 egg whites
6 tablespoons sugar

Add salt to egg whites; beat stiff, but not dry. Continue beating and gradually add sugar, beating until all sugar is added and egg whites stand up in peaks. Spread on fill. Bake in a very hot oven (425 degrees) 5 minutes.

Graham Cracker Crust

20 square Sugar Honey Graham Crackers
¼ cup (½ stick) butter or margarine (let soften to room temperature)
¼ cup sugar

Roll graham crackers to fine even crumbs. Putting crackers in a plastic or cellophane bag, or between two sheets of wax paper prevents scattering and let you see the fineness and uniformity as you go along.

Pour crumbs into bowl. Add soft butter or margarine and sugar. Blend these ingredients well with fingers, fork or pastry blender.

Pour crumb mixture into 9 inch pie plate. Set 8 inch pie plate on top of crumbs and press firmly to make an even layer of crumbs on bottom and sides of 9 inch pie plate. Remove 8 inch pie plate. Crumb Crust shell is now ready to fill as is, to freeze (for ice cream pie) or to bake in a moderately hot oven (375 degrees) for 8 minutes (for a crisper crust and extra delicious flavor).

* * * * *

★ CUSTARD PIE

2 eggs
¼ cup sugar
Speck salt
1½ cup milk, scalded
a little grated nutmeg

Beat the eggs, add the sugar, nutmeg, salt then stir in scalded milk.

Line the plate with pastry, rolled thin. Bake in quick oven at 450 degrees.

* * * * *

FRUIT COCKTAIL PARFAIT PIE

From Homemaker Magazine

1 9-inch baked pastry shell
1 can (17 oz) fruit cocktail
¾ cup water

1 pkg (3 oz) lime flavored gelatin
1 pint vanilla ice cream
Whipping cream

Drain fruit cocktail, reserving syrup. Pour syrup and water into 2 quart saucepan. Bring to boil. Remove from heat. Add gelatin. Stir until dissolved. Cut ice cream into 6 – 8 pieces. Blend into hot gelatin until ice cream is melted. Chill until partially set. Fold in fruit. Pour into pastry shell. Chill to set. Serve with whipped cream.

* * * * *

GRACE HAMILTON PIE

3 cups rhubarb
2 eggs
2 cups sugar
2 tablespoons flour

Beat eggs until thick. Mix flour, sugar and salt together. Add eggs and the flour mixture to rhubarb. Bake between 375 – 400 degrees for 10 minutes then 45 minutes at 350 degrees.

* * * * *

GRANOLA PIE

¾ cup sugar
2 beaten eggs
¾ cup maple-flavored waffle syrup
2/3 cup butter

1 1/3 cups granola
2 teaspoon vanilla
½ cup chopped pecans
1 unbaked pie shell

Mix all ingredients except pecans and pie shell together thoroughly. Pour into pie shell; sprinkle top with nuts. Bake for 30 – 40 minutes at 350 degrees.

* * * * *

IMPOSSIBLE PIE

From Susie Fernstandt

½ cup Bisquick
½ cup sugar
4 eggs
2 cups milk

1 teaspoon vanilla
3 tablespoons oleo
Pinch nutmeg
1 (3 ½ oz) can coconut (½ cup)

Put everything in bowl and mix with mixer. Pour into buttered pie pan. Bake until set (400 degrees for 25-30 minutes.)

* * * * *

LIBBY'S FAMOUS PUMPKIN PIE RECIPE: MAKES 2 PIES

4 eggs, slightly beaten
1 can (29 oz) Libby's Solid Pack Pumpkin
1½ cups sugar
1 teaspoon salt
2 teaspoons ground cinnamon
1 teaspoon ground ginger

½ teaspoon ground cloves
2 cans (12 fl oz ea.) Carnation Evaporated
Milk OR 3 cups half & half

2 9-inch unbaked homemade pie shells
with high fluted edges

Preheat oven to 425 degrees. Combine filling ingredients in order given; divide evenly into pie shells. Bake 15 minutes. Reduce temperature to 350 degrees and bake an additional 45 minutes or until knife inserted near center of piece comes out clean. Cool: garnish, if desired with whipped topping.

* * * * *

★ PUMPKIN DESSERT SQUARE PIE

1 cup flour
½ cup rolled oats
½ cup brown sugar, firmly packed
½ cup butter

Combine until crumbly. Press in 13 x 9 pan and bake at 350 degrees for 15 minutes.

Combine:
1 (1 lb) can solid pack pumpkin
1 (13-oz) condensed milk
2 eggs
¾ cup sugar

½ teaspoon salt
1 teaspoon cinnamon
½ teaspoon ginger
¼ teaspoon cloves

Bake at 350 degrees for 20 – 25 minutes.

Spread over top.
½ cup chopped pecan
½ cup brown sugar
2 tablespoons butter

* * * * *

RAISIN PIE

1½ cups seedless raisins
1½ cups boiling water
grated rind and juice of one lemon

2 tablespoons flour
½ cup sugar
1 tablespoon butter

Cook raisins in boiling water until tender. Mix flour, sugar and butter and add to raisins. Continue to cook and stir until thick. Add lemon rind and juice. Cool slightly and bake between two crusts.

* * * * *

RHUBARB CREAM PIE

Mom (From Chicago Tribune April 27, 1977)

2 tablespoons butter
4 cups fresh rhubarb cut in 1 inch pieces
    (about 1 pound)
1 cup sugar
¼ cup sugar
2 tablespoons cornstarch
3 slightly beaten egg yolks

1/3 cup half & half
1/8 teaspoon salt
Red food coloring (optional)
1 baked 9 in pie shell
3 egg whites
1/3 cup sugar

Melt butter in heavy saucepan. Add rhubarb and 1 cup sugar. Cook slowly, stirring frequently, for 10 minutes, or until rhubarb is tender.

Mix ¼ cup sugar, cornstarch, egg yolks, half & half and salt; add to rhubarb. Cook, stirring constantly until thickened. Add food coloring, if desired. Pour cream filling into cooled pie shell. Beat egg whites until soft peaks form: gradually beat in sugar until stiff peaks form. Pile onto filling, spreading to seal well with edge. Bake at 400 degrees about 10 minutes or until delicately browned.

* * * * *

★ RHUBARB CUSTARD PIE

3 or 4 eggs, slightly beaten
1 tablespoon corn starch
2 cups sugar (Can reduce to 1½ cups)
dash of salt
2 cups rhubarb, cut up (Can increase to 2½ cups)

Crust:

Whip together
½ cup oil
2 Tablespoons milk

Stir in
1½ cup flour
½ teaspoon salt

Put in pie tin.

Bake in 400 degree oven for 50 – 60 minutes.

* * * * *

RHUBARB PIE

From Jean Byrd C

2 cups rhubarb
1½ cups sugar
3 tablespoons corn starch
2 egg yolks

Cook till thick

Put in baked shell and cover with egg whites

* * * * *

RHUBARB PIE

Editor's Note: This was the recipe Granny gave me for rhubarb pie.
3 cups rhubarb
2 eggs
2 cups sugar
2 tablespoons flour
½ teaspoon salt

Beat eggs until thick. Mix flour, sugar and salt together. Add eggs to flour mixture and then add rhubarb. Bake between 375 – 400 degrees for 10 minutes. Then for 45 minutes at 350 degrees.

* * * * *

SODDY RHUBARB PIE

Crust:

1 cup flour
½ cup butter
2 tablespoons sugar

Bake in 350 degree oven 20 – 25 minutes.

Filling:

Cook until thick, stirring often:
1¼ cups sugar
3 beaten egg yolks
2¼ cups rhubarb
1/3 cup cream
2 tablespoons flour

Beat the egg whites and add 1/3 cup sugar. Top pie and brown at 375 degrees.

* * * * *

SUN-COOKED APPLE PIE

Here's a scrumptious dessert that's good nutrition from top to bottom.

1 cup wheat germ	4 cups grated apples
½ cup chopped dates	½ cup honey
¼ cup ground almonds	1 cup yogurt (homemade)

Combine wheat germ, chopped dates and almonds. Mix well and press into a pie plate to be used as pie crust. Combine grated apple and honey and put this into the pie crust. Top with the whipped yogurt and sprinkle with chopped nuts.

* * * *

Candy

FUDGE – 5 LBS.

Note on recipe says: this is the one granny used.
4 cups white sugar
1 large can condensed milk
¼ lb. butter

Place in pan over fire – bring to a boil. Boil 5 minutes stirring constantly.
Remove and add:
1 (12 oz.) Hershey bar
1 cup nuts
2 teaspoons vanilla

Beat until dissolved and add:
 1 jar marshmallow cream (1 pint)

Stir in mixture until blended. Pour into greased pans.

NOTE: Granny used 1 square Bakers Chocolate instead of the 12 oz. Hershey bar and cooked to a soft ball in water, or used a thermometer. Put into 2 9x9 pans.

★ ★ ★ ★ ★

FUDGE CANDY

3 packages (6 oz each) semi-sweet chocolate pieces
1 jar (7 ½ or 8 oz) marshmallow cream
2 cups (½ pound) broken pecans
1 teaspoon vanilla extract
5 cups sugar
½ cup butter
1/8 teaspoon salt
1 tall can (13 oz) evaporated milk

Butter a large pan about 12 x 7½ x 2, or two or more smaller pans. Open the jar of marshmallow cream. Have the pecans ready and loosen vanilla cap for ready measuring. These ingredients need to be added the instant the cooked mixture is removed from the heat.

Into a 4-quart saucepan, measure sugar, then add butter, salt, and evaporated milk. Stirring constantly, cook gently over medium heat to soft ball stage (236 degrees). It takes about 20 minutes from the time the mixture is put on to cook. Remove from heat. Immediately add chocolate, marshmallow cream, pecans, and vanilla. Stir quickly and vigorously until chocolate is melted and all ingredients are well blended. When mixture begins to thicken, turn into buttered pan. When cold, cut into squares.

Makes about 5 pounds.

★ ★ ★ ★ ★

GRANOLA CANDY

1½ cups granola *
1 cup old-fashioned peanut butter
1 cup dark honey
1 cup Shaklee Instant Protein Cocoa Bean
Coconut or nuts

Mix the above ingredients together well and roll in coconuts or nuts in2 log shapes and slice.

*NOTE: See recipe for Basic Granola.

* * * * *

PEANUT BRITTLE

1 cup sugar
½ cup white Karo syrup
½ cup water
2 cups raw peanuts

Generous teaspoon salt
Butter (the size of a walnut)
1 teaspoon baking soda

Boil sugar, syrup, and water in heavy 2 quart saucepan to soft ball stage. Add peanuts and salt. Stir intermittently until syrup turns brown.

Remove from stove. Add butter and stir until melted. Add baking soda and stir until foamy.

Pour onto well-buttered 12x18 inch cookie sheet with four sides, and spread thin by turning sheet from side to side. Cool (takes about a half hour). Break into pieces.

Yield: About 1¼ pounds.

* * * * *

TOFFEE FOR CHRISTMAS

From Mrs. Helen Myers

½ lb butter
1 cup white sugar
sweet chocolate (bars or chunks)
chopped nuts

Melt butter and sugar together. Cook slowly about two minutes. Increase heat and cook for 3 – 4 minutes longer, stirring constantly in one direction. Should be gold brown when done. Pour on heavy wax paper on a bread board or cookie sheet. When cold, loosen from paper, spreading each side with melted sweet chocolate and chopped nuts. First spread one side, let cool, and then the other side. Put in refrigerator for chocolate to harden. Break in pieces.

Recommended to prepare in heavy iron skillet.

* * * * *

Pickles & Relish

APPLE BUTTER

From Jean (Earl's mother)

2 quarts apples
4 cups sugar
2 teaspoons cinnamon
¼ teaspoon cloves

She uses Sure Jell, so you don't have to cook it so long (1 box for this).

★ ★ ★ ★ ★

BARBECUE SAUCE

From Ella E. Copelan, Sweet Home, ORE (Prevention)

It's nice to be able to make your own barbecue sauce. Then you know it has good ingredients and no additives. This one is delicious and tangy.

1 cup tomato puree
1 large tomato
2 tablespoons cold-pressed oil
¼ cup apple cider vinegar

1/8 teaspoon cayenne
3 tablespoons honey
1 medium onion (sliced)
½ green pepper (sliced)

Mix in blender until smooth. Serve on meats, etc. Use as a basting sauce on broiled or roasted meats, or chicken. Keep refrigerated.

★ ★ ★ ★ ★

150

COLD PICKLE RECIPE

From Jean (Earl's Mother)

1 gallon pickles, sliced thin – unpeeled. Soak in salt water overnight.
2 quarts water
¾ cup salt
Drain

Cut fine and add:
1 green pepper
1 red pepper
1 onion

Add
5 cups sugar
5 cups white vinegar
½ teaspoon dill seed
1 teaspoon turmeric
1 teaspoon mustard seed
1 teaspoon celery seed

Mix all together and refrigerate until used. Do not cook or seal. Keeps for 1 year in refrigerator. Left over juice is good for lettuce salad (after pickles are used.)

* * * * *

CRANBERRY-APPLE RELISH

Here is a most delicious sugarless relish to go with turkey, chicken, etc., and made without sugar.

1 pound fresh cranberries
5 pounds apples (preferably mixed – McIntosh, Cortland, yellow Delicious, etc.)
2 cups pineapple juice or apple juice
1 teaspoon cinnamon (optional)

Place in large soup pot washed and picked-over berries, sliced apples, juice and simmer about two hours. Add cinnamon the last half hour.

Relish can be stored in refrigerator for several weeks.

* * * * *

150

LIBERTY PICKLES

From Mrs. Fred Blum

Wash and fill a 2 gallon jar with small cucumbers and sprinkle with 1 pint salt.
Pour on 1 gallon boiling water. Leave on pickles six days. Drain, pour on clear boiling water and let stand 24 hours. Drain again and place 2 tablespoons powdered alum on top of pickles and pour on boiling water. Let stand 24 hours. Drain and split each pickle. Bring to boil the following:
8 cups sugar
2½ quarts vinegar
2 tablespoons celery seed
1 tablespoon mustard seed
a few pieces cinnamon bark
a small handful of horseradish (optional)

Pour over pickles in jar. Drain and reheat liquid each day for four days, then put over pickles and lay a plate on top. No weight and no canning.
The horseradish may be left out.
Be sure to cut each pickle.

* * * * *

PICKLES

From Jean

6 cups cucumber, sliced
1 cup onions, sliced
¼ cup salt
1 cup vinegar
2 cups sugar
1 teaspoon celery seed
1 teaspoon mustard seed

Combine cucumber and onion. Cover with water. Add salt and stir; refrigerate 2 hours. Drain salt water. Add vinegar, sugar and seeds. Refrigerate.

* * * * *

152

★ PICKLE BEETS

From Janet (Mrs. Will Hartwig)

Very Good

Boil syrup of
3 cups sugar
2 cups vinegar
1 scant teaspoon salt
1 tablespoon mixed spices in clothe bag

Then heat beets to boiling point in syrup and can.

* * * * *

RHUBARB JELLY 'GOO'

From Jean

Mix and let stand overnight at room temperature:
5 cups chopped rhubarb, cut fine
3 cups sugar

In the morning, cook until thick.
Add 1 3 oz pkg strawberry Jell-O. Stirring until dissolved.

Can be put in jars or Tupperware containers and freeze till ready to use.

* * * * *

SAUSAGE STUFFING

Turkey giblets and neck
1/2 bay leaf
1/2 teaspoon salt
1 teaspoon salt
2 cups boiling water
3 celery ribs with leaves
6 cups bread crumbs (made from day old bread)

3 tablespoons onion, finely chopped
3 tablespoons parsley, chopped
3/4 teaspoon pepper or paprika
6 tablespoons melted butter
3/4 pound pork sausage meat
1½ cup celery, chopped
1 cup chestnuts, chopped (optional)

* * * * *

TOMATOE JAM

1 lemon cut up – cook in ¼ cup water until clear.
Add tomatoes and SureJell

* * * * *

TWENTY DAY PICKLES

From Violet

Put pickles in brine strong enough to float an egg. Let stand 9 days. Stir once in a while. Then wash and drain and put them in alum water for 2 days using 2 level teaspoons of powdered alum to 1 gallon of water. After 2 days, drain and cover with cold white vinegar. Let stand 9 days again.

Now make a rich syrup, using the same vinegar.

1 cup vinegar
2 cups sugar
1 teaspoon oil of cloves
½ teaspoon oil of cinnamon

Pack pickles in jar and pour this liquid over – after it is cold.

* * * * *

WESTPORT CRANBERRY RELISH

From Jean

3 cups fresh, whole cranberries
1 orange unpeeled, quartered and seeded
1 tart apple, unpeeled, cored and
    quartered
¾ cup sugar

1/8 teaspoon salt
¼ teaspoon cinnamon
½ cup golden seedless raisins
½ cup chopped dried apricots
½ cup chopped pecans

Coarsely grind first three ingredients. Stir in sugar, salt and cinnamon. Set aside. Cook raisins and apricots in ½ cup water over medium heat until raisins are plump; about 5 – 10 minutes; drain. Stir raisins, apricots and pecans into relish. Refrigerate overnight to allow flavors to blend. Yields approximately 3½ cups relish.

* * * * *

ZUCCHINI RELISH

From Earl's Mother

Chop fine, put through coarse knife of food chopper:
6 cups zucchini
1 onion
1 green pepper
1 red pepper

Cover with 3 tablespoons salt and cold water. Let stand 3 hours and then drain well.

Then add:
3 cups sugar
2 cups white vinegar
1 tablespoon celery seed

Boil 10 minutes and seal

* * * * *

SNACKS & MISC

APRICOT MARBLES

From Mrs. B. H. Weeks Everett, WA

The kids will enjoy rolling these – right into their eager mouths.

1 cup sun dried apricots
½ cut nut meats
½ pound coconut
4 tablespoons lemon juice

Put apricots, nut meats and coconut through a food grinder. Add lemon juice, shape into balls and roll in grated nuts. Refrigerate.

* * * * *

BASIC GRANOLA

2 cups rolled oats
¼ cup wheat germ
¼ cup sesame seeds
¼ cup shredded coconut

¼ cup sunflower seeds
3 ½ tablespoons oil
¼ cup honey
1 teaspoon salt

In bowl, mix all of the above except the oil, honey and salt. In small bowl, combine oil, honey and salt and add very slowly to the dry mixture, mixing with a spoon or two forks until completely coated.

In a 9 x 12 cake pan, spread out the granola and bake in slow (300 degree) oven until golden brown. Watch carefully; it can burn suddenly. Let cool; as it cools it becomes crisp. Store in refrigerator.

NOTE: Nuts, raisins, etc, may be added to suit your taste.

* * * * *

OAT-CORN CRUMBLES

From Laura Whitson Mulberry, ARK

These are delicious as a substitute for crackers in soup or as a cereal. You can bake a large amount and freeze the cooled crumbles. This way they are ready for immediate use.

2 2/3 cups oatmeal
1/3 cup wheat germ
1 cup whole grain cornmeal
¾ teaspoon sea salt
2 tablespoons honey

1 tablespoon each sesame and sunflower
   seeds
3 tablespoons oil
2/3 cup hot water
¼ cup coarsely shredded coconut

Mix well oatmeal, wheat germ, cornmeal, sea salt, and seeds.

In large bowl put oil and honey. Mix. Add hot water. Mix well. Add coconut.

Pour bowl of dry ingredients into wet ingredients. Mix well, till crumbly.

Place in large oiled pan. Bake at 350 degrees for 1½ hours, more or less, or until brown and crisp. Stir occasionally while baking.

* * * * *

POTATO FLOUR NOODLES

From a newspaper.

An easy way to make your own nutritious noodles.

3 eggs
3 tablespoons water
3 tablespoons potato flour
1/8 teaspoon sea salt

Beat eggs; add water, salt and flour. Blend well; it makes a thin batter. Heat a small frying pan (6 or 7 inches) brush with peanut or safflower oil. Pour 1 tablespoon of the batter in a thin stream starting at the center and tilt the pan to distribute evenly.

Cook over moderate heat on both sides till lightly browned. Turn on a towel. When cool, roll up each pancake and cut very thin. They are delicious with chicken soup. No cooking needed.

I have to hide them from my children and grandchildren or they eat them up before we are ready for the meal.

* * * * *

RAW AFTER SCHOOL SNACKS

From: Mrs. Lillian W. Benson – Manistee, MI

These luscious roll gems will delight the children and give them good nutrients at the same time.

1 cup raw wheat germ
½ cup soy grits
1 cup soy lecithin granules
½ cup date sugar
½ cup organic honey
1 cup carob powder
1 cup grated fresh coconut

½ cup sesame or sunflower seed oil
2 teaspoons vanilla
1½ cup chopped dates
1 cup seedless raisins
1 cup sunflower meal or sesame meal or
    almond meal

Mix dry ingredients; add oil, honey and vanilla. Add to dry mixture. Add dates, raisins, coconut and sesame meal. Mix with enough good water to be able to lightly knead the mixture. Divide it in thirds. Sprinkle coconut on sheet of wax paper and shape into a 1½ x 10 inch roll. Store the rolls in the refrigerator. Then cut small portion off to make individual rolls.

* * * * *

STUFFED FRUIT

From: R.Warden – Lenoir, NC

Here's a delicious snack that will satisfy your sweet tooth and give you sustained energy. Pack a few in the children's lunch boxes when they go on hikes for a morale and energy boost.

1 cup unsulphured raisins
1 cup shredded coconut
¾ cup sunflower seed or nutmeats (or mixture)
1 tablespoon lemon juice (more or less as needed)
Dried prunes, slightly cooked and drained
Pitted dates
Dried apricots, slightly cooked and drained
Put raisins, coconut and nuts or seeds through grinder. Blend with lemon juice. Use about ½ teaspoon to stuff prunes, dates and apricots.

* * * * *

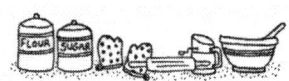

SUNBURGERS

These burgers pack a lot of good-tasting nutrition into a small space. Great for a lunch box.

1 cup ground sunflower seeds
½ cup grated raw carrots
½ cup celery, chopped fine
2 tablespoons chopped onion
1 tablespoon chopped parsley
1 egg

1 tablespoon Soya oil
½ teaspoon sea salt
1 tablespoon green pepper, chopped
¼ cup tomato juice
1 pinch of basil

Combine with enough tomato juice so the patties hold a good shape. Arrange in a shallow baking dish and bake at 350 degrees until browned. Turn and brown on the other side.

* * * * *

SUNSHINE SPREAD

A nice change from peanut butter. Keep it in the refrigerator. Let the children help themselves. It's great on sliced apples.

1 cup wheat germ
2 cups honey
1 cup sunflower seed meal
1 cup pumpkin seed meal

Shake dry ingredients in wide mouth Mason jar to distribute evenly. Cut in honey with knife, or tighten cap and turn jar sufficient times for honey to be absorbed thoroughly.

* * * * *

Made in the USA
Lexington, KY
23 June 2017